LISP
The Language of Artificial Intelligence

LISP

The Language of Artificial Intelligence

A. A. Berk

 VAN NOSTRAND REINHOLD COMPANY

New York

LL

Library of Congress Catalog Card Number: 85–20172
ISBN: 0–442–20974–6

Manufactured in the United States of America

Published by Van Nostrand Company Inc.
115 Fifth Avenue
New York, New York 10003

Van Nostrand Reinhold Company Limited
Molly Millars Lane
Wokingham, Berkshire RG11 2PY, England

Van Nostrand Reinhold
480 Latrobe Steeet
Melbourne, Victoria 3000, Australia

Macmillan of Canada
Division of Gage Publishing Limited
164 Commander Boulevard
Agincourt, Ontario MIS 3C7, Canada

15 14 13 12 11 10 9 8 7 6 5 4 3 2 1

Library of Congress Cataloging–in–Publication Data

Berk, A. A.
   LISP, the language of artificial intelligence.

   Includes index.
   1. LISP (Computer program language)   2. Artificial
intelligence.   I. Title.
QA76.73.L23B47 1985   006.3   85–20172
ISBN 0–442–20974–6

Contents

Preface

As large numbers of computer companies become committed to the fifth generation of machines, it is likely that just as everyone today knows what a word processor is, very soon the expert system will be a part of everyone's lives. Already, such commercial uses for artificial intelligence research are in general use, and industry is slowly becoming aware of intelligent uses for the computing machine other than simply making the process of writing letters easier.

Along with artificial intelligence itself, a whole gamut of hardware and software tools has sprung up, from speech processors to special languages. This book is largely concerned with one of the latter. Several important languages have grown up with our desire to invest machinery with intelligence, and one of the most popular, and easy to learn, is LISP.

As you will see, throughout this book AI is concerned with the manipulation of lists of objects. Thus, a good AI language must be concerned primarily with lists and their manipulation. To give a short answer to the question as to why this is so, just consider that a sentence, or any collection of words, such as this book for instance, is nothing more than a list. Within that list there is a large amount of structure, and it is this structure which LISP is good at manipulating.

Throughout the book examples are given to ensure that you learn the language from a practical point of view. The last chapter contains an example of a longer LISP program which is orientated towards AI, and gives an example of a learning process. AI is a young subject, and as such there is still tremendous scope for anyone to press the frontiers forward in some small or large way. You should bear this in mind as you read through.

It is always useful to base a book of this type on a common and available standard, and much of the work you will find here is compatible with Acornsoft's LISP. However, this is a fairly general dialect, and you should have no difficulty with other versions.

I should like to thank my wife for her continuous support and assistance during the gruelling business of late nights, continuous coffee and my total distraction from family life. I should also like to thank my father for giving up his computer equipment for the entire duration of the preparation of this book, so that I could run LISP on one machine, and type into the other.

A. A. Berk

LISP
The Language of Artificial Intelligence

Chapter One
Introduction to Artificial Intelligence

Introduction

This book is aimed at giving the reader a primer in a language which is at the centre of a new revolution in computing. This revolution is based on the concept of giving machines intelligence, and the subject involved is called 'artificial intelligence' – AI for short.

There are many reasons for pursuing this line of study, apart from the fact that it is inherently interesting. For instance, analysing the basis of intelligence can teach us more about ourselves, and the way we think. Another important reason concerns the industrial uses of computers. It is generally accepted that the more human-like the machine, the more acceptable and understandable it will be. The aim is to produce a generation of machines which will communicate with us by natural speech and hearing, use human vision, and be capable of creative intelligence. By these means it should be possible to mass-produce machines which will finally be capable of being useful intelligent companions in both work and play.

As you can see, the tie-up between artificial intelligence and robotics is clear and essential. In robotics we try to invent the mechanical devices to which artificial intelligence programs will be applied. Of course, the concept of the clever robot is one to which we have all been exposed for decades. The task of producing such machinery is almost 'old hat'. The only problem is that science moves more slowly than our imagination! However, the gap between science fiction and fact is closing, and we are now in an era of great expansion in the realms of the intelligent machine, and perhaps the greatest problem is to invent the necessary programming structures. After all, mechanics is an ancient subject; programming is a mere 'babe-in-arms' in comparison.

Computer language

It is generally recognised that a corner-stone of the programming task is the correct choice of computer language. There are several main candidates at present, and LISP is the most widely known. (Another is a language called PROLOG, which has many similarities to LISP.) The word LISP comes from List Processing, and we shall see shortly how essential the manipulation of quantities called 'lists' is to the study of artificial intelligence.

LISP is different from the BASIC-like languages in a number of ways, and it is fair to ask the question 'Why bother to change one's tack, and learn a new language?'. Unfortunately, this can only be answered *fully* by learning that new language! However, before examining LISP, this chapter aims to give the reader a short grounding in the main application of LISP (i.e. artificial intelligence), and demonstrate how cumbersome BASIC is for this task. This will show why a new language is worth learning, and what sort of attributes it should have.

What you need to know

The following assumes that the reader understands the meaning of the words 'computer program', along with the most common BASIC keywords. It is important that some programming has been attempted, so that important concepts such as logical thinking, sequential processing, and breaking a problem down into modules have already been learned by experience. No detailed or deep knowledge is assumed, and this book is quite suitable for relative beginners and experienced programmers alike.

Intelligence in general

A universal fact about the study of intelligence is that no matter who you ask, they will have a view as to what intelligence actually is. This is quite natural for two reasons. Firstly, we all possess it, and secondly there is no complete definition of intelligence, and everyone's view is equally valid.

There have been, of course, attempts at a definition, and one such will be given later. However, an important fact about AI research is that human intelligence must be broken into small parts, and each one considered separately.

For instance, it does not seem impossible to produce machinery which can learn a set of facts, and answer questions on a given subject. This is a part of AI called *Expert Systems*.

The problem of playing games is a very advanced part of AI research – we have all seen the remarkable sophistication of chess programs. Video games are highly complex intelligent programs aimed at testing our mental resources to the limit.

A large area of AI looks at the possible analysis of natural language to produce intelligent speech. This is not simply a matter of making sounds which are realistic, a problem which has now been cracked. The main problem is to make the computer understand sentence structure, and be capable of generating its own.

These are some of the main areas of modern AI research. However, if you consider the true meaning of human intelligence, you will quickly see how inadequate these topics are. They do not address the problems of human learning, with our ability to recognise a given object in almost any context. They do not look at the complex emotional and irrational aspects of our mental abilities. They do not attack the problem of giving machines creativity, or lateral thought. Finally, they do not consider the remarkable ability of humans to conceptualise. This is such a deep area that it does not even presently have a definition and leads us into the realms of psychology. Furthermore, the idea of giving a machine consciousness is forbidding, and contemplation of this possibility has produced a vast industry of horror and science fiction.

This book will be confined to a few of the simpler AI topics which are being investigated today, as well as aiming to give you a good grounding in an important AI language.

Communication

One of the first stages in the study of giving intelligence to machines is to grasp the fact that communication is at the basis of the subject. There are several reasons for this. Primarily, we find it difficult (though not impossible) to gauge the intelligence of a man or machine with whom we cannot easily communicate. This is a basic human trait which is deeply ingrained. We have all had the experience of talking down to people who cannot speak our own language, as if they were of lower intelligence. This is generally due to our habit of taking for granted the remarkable sophistication and depth of even the simplest of communication. Think of how much subtlety and nuance there is locked up in a phrase as simple as:

'Chance would be a fine thing'

And if you think that is easy, try explaining it to a highly intelligent man who only understands your own language to the level of a child!

Another reason for the importance of communication as the basis of AI is that the complexity, or rather subtlety, of the communication method is a good indicator of intelligence. Much of our own intelligence is irrevocably bound up with the way in which we use words. An example of this is in the concept of the 'joke'. It is often the clever or surprising way in which words are used which constitutes the 'punchline'. In this, and many other areas, the most poorly educated people use words in a manner which is incomparably more intelligent than that of even the most intelligent members of the animal kingdom. The subtlety of natural language indicates our intelligence, and its distinction from that of the other animals.

Another aspect of the role of communication in intelligence is in the human's possession of a 'mind's eye'. It is this 'consciousness' which appears to set us apart from other animals. Most people will admit that though a part of one's thought is in patterns and pictures, there is a large fraction which is entirely in words. The way in which mankind has manufactured an elaborate and widespread variety of communication systems between man and man is not a bad indication of high intelligence within a species.

Assessing intelligence

As mentioned above, an important aspect of intelligence is that everyone has a feeling as to what constitutes intelligence. There is no accepted definition of this elusive quality, yet we can all recognise it. This has an important consequence. It means that anyone can 'dabble' in the study of intelligence. There is no reason why the enthusiast should not be able to make some interesting inroads into the subject by himself – the field is open to all.

Another important point is that it is interesting to analyse how we do make an assessment of someone's intelligence. If you think about this you will discover that communication is often the most important part of the assessment. People who appear eloquent, or authoritative, are labelled by others as intelligent. This can, of course, be an illusion – an important point which also applies to the apparent intelligence of machines.

A good way to start an attempt at a definition of intelligence is to ask the simple question: 'How would one assess the intelligence or otherwise of an alien met under circumstances which did not give any clue as to his natural intelligence?'. Thus, if we met the alien after he had landed on Earth, we would have to call him intelligent, unless we believed he was a test animal sent by another race, and had no part in the intelligent activity of building or piloting a space-ship across the interstellar void!

It is, of course, in science fiction that we find this type of question discussed in many intricate forms. A typical scenario is one where an Earth space-ship finds an alien ship on its travels. The alien ship contains a large and exotic zoo in its holds, and apparently no crew. The conclusion is drawn that the crew have taken the intelligent step of realising that one exotic creature will look very much like another, and have simply taken to the cages along with their cargo. This is presumably an attempt to prevent the apparently invading humans from torturing the alien's home-star coordinates from them. The (naturally) peace-loving humans merely wish to establish friendly communications, and set about trying to find out which creatures are intelligent. This is where a definition of intelligence is required.

The obvious test, of course, is to establish any kind of communication, even if unreciprocated by the other side. This then gives the humans a chance to convince the aliens of their friendly intentions.

One might argue that whether the aliens can do higher mathematics, or build anti-gravity machines is less important than the simple act of communication. However, it should also be mentioned that for establishing common ground between alien races, the principles of the simplest universal mathematical laws are often argued to be a good place to start.

The main theme of the above is to suggest that communication is all-important within intelligence of any kind.

Intelligent communication

There are many aspects to AI, but the popular, and most common concept of AI in the majority of people's minds is the ability of a computing machine to 'talk' to humans in their own language. The more creative and 'intelligent-seeming' this 'speech', the more intelligent seems the machine. This also leads to some interesting anomalies.

In the field of AI, researchers are continuously trying to analyse the way in which natural spoken languages can be used by machines. The interesting consequence of this research is that a very simple program can appear highly intelligent to even well educated people.

This is due to a well known human trait called 'anthropomorphisation'. To 'anthropomorphise' something is to imbue it with apparent human traits. For instance, many of us consider our pets to be 'almost human'. We constantly assume that some gesture of a purely instinctive kind is human in some sense. Many people talk to their pets in a fairly serious manner, and give the animal apparent answers of a human kind. It is a natural trait within us not to hurt their feelings by saying things in front of them which would hurt a human's feelings, and so on. In a similar way, we use the pronoun 'she' for ships, countries, veteran cars and so on, more often than 'it'.

This anthropomorphic trait within us all can be used to good effect by a simple program which is able to manipulate language in a purely mechanical way. For instance, it is not difficult to construct a program which has a fairly large vocabulary, and can turn questions and statements input by the user around, and fire them back. For instance, the user might type in a sentence such as:

'I think you are unintelligent'

'I think' is a common way to introduce a statement, and this could lead the computer to pick out the main words in the subsequent clause. The subsequent clause asserts something about the computer, and it might be programmed to take statements about itself, look at its vocabulary, and if it finds an uncomplimentary adjective, print out a response of the following form:

'You should think more carefully before using words such as "unintelligent".'

or:

> 'Don't call me "unintelligent" before considering your own position!'

This type of apparently considered and slightly aggressive response will generally surprise people, and put them on their mettle. This is a perfect position from which to convince them of the intelligence of the machine. As long as the machine never actually becomes tongue-tied, and does not repeat its responses too often, the human will imagine a considerably greater intelligence within the computer than is really the case.

The idea, therefore, is to stick to a standard type of reply, and perhaps vary it slightly and randomly for each occurrence. This 'algorithm' is easy to incorporate in a simple program, and it will surprise most people who use the system.

Another simple rule is to produce deliberate misdirections, or vague ambiguous statements in response to questions which are not 'understood' by the program. Such ploys are often used by people to save them from having to answer a question properly in a given situation. For instance, a response to a question might be:

> 'You ask such provocative questions'

or

> 'The answer to this type of question is deeper than you think'

Other simple rules might include the turning around of the 'person' of a statement. For instance, you might type in:

> 'My name is George'

The automatic response could be:

> 'Your name is George'

The idea throughout is to disguise the lack of intelligent consideration of the essence of the input sentences by straightforward automatic responses. These are selected according to a simple algorithm. A random selection element may also be thrown in for good measure to prevent continuous repetition of exactly the same words.

Some of these rules, and others, have been used to explore human reaction to machine intelligence. Probably the best known was constructed in the early years of AI research and called *Eliza*.

Eliza exists in many forms, both large and small, and is nothing more than a set of mechanical response mechanisms. It should be obvious that the constructor of the program would be able to predict the outcome of any operator input, at least in essence, from his intimate knowledge. Such straightforward predictability could almost be taken as a definition of *un*intelligence. It was with some concern, therefore, that AI researchers noted the remarkably detailed and meaningful conversations which even highly 'intelligent' people were seen to conduct with this program. This example shows how very subjective the meaning of machine intelligence actually is.

The Turing test

Many attempts have been made to define intelligence, and such attempts would take us beyond the scope of this book. However, there is one simple intelligence test which is worth appreciating, as it provides food for thought while experimenting with your own programs. It is another attempt to solve the 'alien intelligence' problem in a slightly different form: how could you be sure that a visiting alien was not a simple robot which had been programmed in English? Or, in computer terms, how do you know when you have invented the ultimately intelligent machine?

A famous researcher named Turing suggested a possible test. A human being is placed within a closed room, and the machine or alien placed in another, so that they are completely separated from each other, and neither can be seen from the outside. They are able to communicate with the outside through a VDU-like channel, capable only of passing words – no sounds or expressions. A series of humans would then simply be allowed to communicate with each of them. The machine or alien would be passed as intelligent if outside observers were unable to tell which was human and which was machine.

This test (the Turing test) has some problems associated with it. It is important, for instance, for the human to be committed to the experiment to the extent that he tries his best to prove himself more intelligent than the machine. However, it is a good idea to compare the machine with a human in some manner, as this is the only template we really have of intelligence. This begs the question, of course, as to whether there are other forms of intelligence, of a non-human kind, which are just as valid. However, for the moment we have enough on our plate to define our own intelligence.

Of course, it is perfectly possible for a number of simple game-playing computer programs to pass the Turing test, when restricted to that game alone. Thus, in a restricted sense, it is possible to pass the Turing test already. The classical example given in this context is the remarkable sophistication of chess-playing computers, which most ordinary chess players would find difficult to recognise as a machine, except, perhaps, by the response time or some other purely mechanical attribute.

Artificial intelligence applications

It is fair to say that most people would admit that their concept of artificial intelligence is one of a human-language-speaking computer, able to hold an interesting conversation. This relies on the ability to perform tasks such as recognising words in context, and pattern matching. This is an area which has to be attacked with a language which is orienatated towards the processing of lists.

Two other areas, mentioned above, of modern AI which are worth exploring are those of *games playing*, and *expert systems*.

Games playing starts with simple games such as noughts and crosses, where a machine can be just as good as a human. This leads on to large and complex strategy games, where the computer is really only an adjunct to the human participants, and is used to set up surprises, and clues, and act as umpire. Computer simulation might be put into this class. It is debatable as to whether this type of application is really intelligence, and most people would demand some creative strategy within the program before calling it intelligent.

'Expert systems' are fast becoming one of the most important industrial applications of AI, and as such will form an increasing part of our everyday life. An expert system is simply an intelligent filing cabinet (or 'database') of information which has been gleaned from an expert in a given field, and stored in a computer.

The classical example, which is disturbing to some, is that of the medical diagnosis system. As much of a GP's diagnostic knowledge as possible is input into a large file, and indexed in a special manner to ensure that it is fully retrievable as required. The system then asks the patient a number of questions, and from the answers asks other more specialised questions. The answers to these questions are analysed according to the GP's normal method of diagnosis, and a result thus formed. The result, in the ideal case, will be a medical opinion as efficient and reliable as that the GP used as the base for the data. This cannot be said to have been achieved quite yet!

Even though the ultimate expert system is not quite here yet, it is true to say that there are many expert systems which act as an aid to the human user. After all, an intelligent, but not perfect, assistant with the advantage of total recall, can be a great asset.

Expert systems and data structure

Technically, the database (or 'knowledge base') which forms the residual expertise of the system is best stored in a manner which links the parts of the information together in an intelligently related form. For instance, it would be perfectly possible to index all the data alphabetically. However, to continue the medical example for a moment, there is no connection between smallpox and smoker's cough, though they might appear near to each other in an alphabetic 'filing cabinet'. Diagnosing illness is clearly not a simple matter of sorting data into alphabetical order. It would be a good idea to analyse how diagnosis is performed, and store the data accordingly.

This connection between the program's goal and the storage of data is one of the most important in AI. It is also, incidentally, one of the main tenets of 'structured programming'. In fact, if you have studied structured programming, you will find that LISP tends, in general, to force structuring in programming.

The correct storage of data leads on to a study of 'data structures', which refers to the manner by which data is stored and indexed, and describes how one piece of data leads on to the position within memory of another.

To see how this is done, we will look at a system for helping a user track down a particular heavenly body such as a star or planet from a mass of given data.

Figure 1.1 shows an example of a simple data structure, not surprisingly called a 'tree'. As you can see, the data is a set of characteristics about

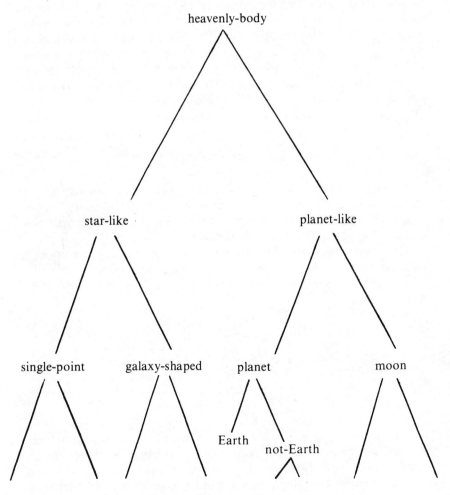

Fig. 1.1 Tree data structures

heavenly bodies in general. It might have been taken from a simple book on the characteristics of commonly known celestial objects. The actual level of the user is important in determining the type of data stored. If the user is to be an astronomer, for instance, it might contain statements about 'albedo', 'density' and 'spectral class'. The whole structure might then be used as an intelligent filing cabinet for astronomical facts.

The tree of characteristics is constructed to show the way in which a program may be written to use the data. The program implied could be a guessing 'game' used to find the name of one of the common heavenly bodies. It would ask relevant questions, and take a path through the tree which would lead to the answer in a short and very human-like manner.

The most important point about Figure 1.1 is that though it looks like a flow-diagram, it is, in fact, just the equivalent of a DATA statement or string array in BASIC. However, the structure shown here, whereby each piece of data actually points to the next in a logical sequence, is not naturally available in the storage methods of BASIC. It must be constructed piecemeal. The power of this type of data structure (the way in which the data is stored) is that it actually implies the form of the associated program.

Let us now see how the structure of Figure 1.1 might be set up and used in BASIC. This will only be done superficially to introduce the main points, otherwise we will be led away from the main point.

The star and planet guessing program

The game is straightforward, but illustrates the ideas behind a very simple expert system. The operator sits in front of the machine, and answers yes or no questions until the program comes to a final end of a tree-branch, such as Earth in Figure 1.1. The program ends there.

One possible program method might simply be to store every possible solution in an array A$(I), in no particular order, and sequence through the array, putting name after name onto the screen, until the operator answers 'yes' to the question:

```
    .
    .
    .
PRINT "Are you thinking of ";A$(I);" ?"
INPUT "Yes or No ?", ANS$
    .
    .
    .
```

This can hardly be considered intelligent, and will soon become both tedious and slow as the number of objects becomes large. In addition, it requires you to know the answer and recognise it. The main idea of an expert system is that the computer asks you a series of questions, and then *it* tells *you* the answer.

A better approach is to start by assuming that we already have the structure of Figure 1.1, and worry about setting it up later. We could then construct the following type of program:

(1) Start at the top of the tree. Tell the operator that this is a program about heavenly bodies. Retrieve the items pointed to by the next two branches (star-like, and planet-like).
(2) Ask which of these two items is applicable. Follow that branch in the tree.
(3) If this is the end of a branch, and there are no further branches, the answer has been found and is printed out.
(4) If there is no answer yet, look along two branches from the present position, and retrieve that data; then go to (2) above.

The data shown in Figure 1.1 implies the simple program above by virtue of its structure. The next problem is how to store all these branches and pointers in a computer. The program itself is the simplest part! If the data has been stored correctly, it will contain much of the 'cleverness' of the system.

The heavenly body data storage

We shall see shortly that LISP is specially designed to store all data in the form diagrammed in Figure 1.1. However, it is instructive to see how we might perform this type of storage in BASIC. It gives a good example of the activities needed in BASIC for this type of application.

A DATA statement would not be suitable for storing the data for a number of reasons. One is that the tree's branches would be difficult to extend in a straightforward manner. The main reason, however, is that a DATA statement contains almost no structure to help the programming; it is simply a linear sequence of items.

The correct way to store the data is in an array. Consider the 2-dimensional array:

   TREE\$ (PAIR, POS)

Here the dimension variables have been chosen to suggest their use. For instance, star-like and planet-like could be thought of as the second pair in the tree, and PAIR would have the value 2 for these two strings. Star-like occupies the first position in the pair, and POS thus has the value 1 for this entry. POS is 2 for planet-like (see Figure 1.2). As you can see, there are as many entries in the array TREE\$ as there are nodes in the tree. A 'node' is simply the meeting point of two branches. You can also see that each pair emanating from a previous node has the same value for PAIR – this variable may be used to label that pair uniquely.

This prescription certainly stores all the information, and even allow pairs

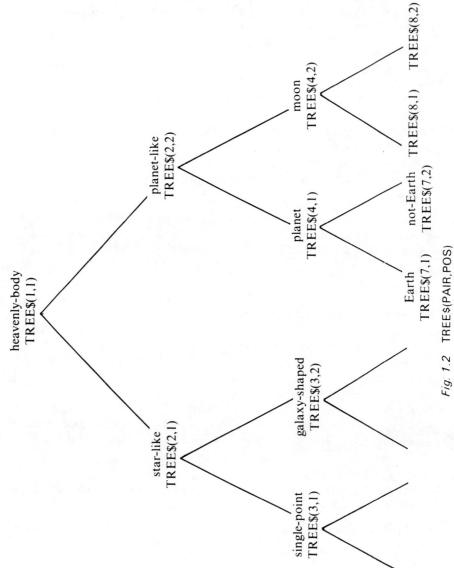

Fig. 1.2 TREE$(PAIR,POS)

of nodes with a common predecessor to be associated together. But, does it encapsulate the total tree structure, so that a program can pick its way through the tree as detailed above? The answer is actually 'no'.

For instance, there is no general natural pointer in this array from

    TREE\$(2,2)   (which equals planet-like)

to:

    TREE\$(4,1)   and   **TREE\$(4,2)**   (planet and moon)

The reason for this is that there is no natural connection between the different values of the *first dimension* of TREE\$. There is no linking from one level to the next down. For instance, (see Figure 1.2) how could you tell from the array alone that TREE\$(4,1) led to TREE\$(7,1) and TREE\$(7,2)?

A linked list

A linked list is a list of items, each of which points to the next, wherever it may be stored. Thus the list can be stored any how, and its structure remains intact, and can be added to easily. Figure 1.2 is a good visual data structure, but is not efficient in computer terms. To add anything in, you will have to rub out bits, and cram the new data in as best as you can. In a linked list, new data is simply stored at the end of the list, and the links, or pointers, are used to define its position within the data structure.

What is needed here is some method of encoding, within the array TREE\$, where the next two branches go from any given node. At the same time, it would be useful to allow for more than two branches from a given node. This can be done by adding more values to POS, for each PAIR value, and using these extra array elements to store pointers to the next elements in the tree, however many there are.

We will stick to 2 branches here, and this gives four array elements for each value PAIR in TREE\$. Each of these two extra values could contain the values of PAIR in the next two pairs. For instance, in Figure 1.2:

```
TREE$(4,1) = "planet"
TREE$(4,2) = "moon"
TREE$(4,3) = "7"
TREE$(4,4) = "8"
```

Thus to find the successor of planet (PAIR=4 POS=1) simply add 2 to its POS value, and look at TREE\$ for that value, which is:

    TREE\$(4,3) = "7"

and this gives the PAIR of the next pair in the tree which will thus be TREE\$(7,1) and TREE\$(7,2). Figure 1.3 shows the tree of Figure 1.2 written in this form.

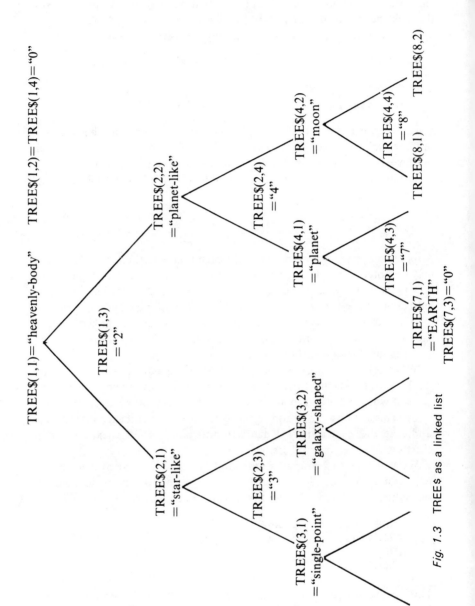

Fig. 1.3 TREE$ as a linked list

This is by no means the only method of structuring the data, and in fact it is not even necessarily the best. You should try to think of other methods for yourself, using arrays. One of the most important points to remember is that it is essential to be able to extend the base of data, along any branch within the tree, in a consistent manner.

Two programs can now be written for this database, in order to give a simple expert system, or guessing game. The first program would be a routine for filling TREE$ with data. It should never be forgotten that in any database, the first task is to create, and be able to update, the database itself. The second program is the game to guess the heavenly body itself.

The BASIC routines

We will now examine, very briefly, the general type of programming needed for this example. The actual program details are a little involved, and take us off the main course of this book. The point about the following is that, in BASIC, it is perfectly possible to set up this type of data structure, but it is not particularly easy or natural.

Data types

There are three different data types to be considered before the programs can be constructed.

First, there is the 'head' of the tree, which is element TREE$(1,1). This contains the word "heavenly-body". There is no companion to this piece of data to reside in TREE$(1,2), and this will be set to "0" to signal this fact (see Figure 1.3). However, there is a pair of branches from TREE$(1,1). Thus, adding 2 to the second dimension, TREE$(1,3) contains the necessary value, "2", for finding the next branches. As TREE$(1,2) leads nowhere, TREE$(1,4) can be set to "0" to signify this fact, for consistency.

The next type of data is the set of descriptions which forms the main body of the tree. This is simply the pairs themselves, as described above.

The final type of data is the type which ends a series of branches – such as "Earth". There are no subsequent branches, and this constitutes an answer to the guessing problem, when reached. It is important that such data can be identified by the program. A method of doing this is simply to store "0" in the array element which would normally store the value for the next two branches. This can be seen in Figure 1.3, where TREE$(7,1) contains "Earth", and TREE$(7,3) contains "0".

This describes the data in sufficient detail to construct both a data-filing program, and a guessing game.

The programs

If you have done some BASIC programming, you will probably be able to construct the programs for yourself. The first program must be capable of filling TREE$ from scratch, as well as adding new data. This will have INPUT statements, and will have to generate the values for POS and PAIR as it runs. Also, when new data is to be input, it will have to generate new, and unused, values of POS to fit the new data into the linked list.

To play the game, the routine outlined above for playing the game can be coded. When a particular answer is being searched for, the program starts at the head of the tree, and asks YES NO questions to determine the next branch to follow. The next branch's POS value is conveniently stored as shown in Figure 1.3. If the dialect of BASIC being used cannot convert strings such as "7" to a numeric value, 7, then this will have to be simulated. The program knows it has ended when adding 2 to the current POS value yields a part of TREE$ which contains 0.

You can see that the entire data structure must be constructed with almost no special help from the language of BASIC. All the data is treated unintelligently as values of string variables. The linking itself has to be put in by the programmer.

Once the complexity of the data structure has been solved, the programming is simple. The principle which comes from this example is that if the data is already structured, one can concentrate on the really important activity – that of constructing intelligent programs.

LISP and similar languages provide a natural structuring to the data. This means that programs can be written in a manner which allows the programmer to 'forget' the background 'housekeeping' task of structuring the list. He can concentrate upon what to do with the list itself.

List-orientated languages

The first part of this chapter explained how important communication and natural human language are in AI. Natural language is composed of lists of words, and thus a computer language which treats lists in a special way will automatically be applicable to human language. The majority of common languages tend to give numbers and algebraic variables more importance than lists or strings. Let us consider some of the attributes of a list-orientated language which would be useful.

An attribute which BASIC does not generally have is automatic recognition of the 'space' character which we all use to separate words in our written language. Thus, as far as BASIC is concerned, a string of characters containing words is a single entity, and not a set of groups of letters separated by spaces. This makes BASIC less useful for manipulating natural language.

Another facility which would be useful would be for the language to store lists of words, automatically, with a certain degree of structure or hierarchy. The tree diagrams above represent such a hierarchy, so that "heavenly-body" is at the top, with "star-like" and "planet-like" on the same (next) level, and so on. We shall see, shortly, that LISP does exactly this.

We have already seen a BASIC string array method of representing a tree diagram, which was constructed by the programmer. A list-orientated language should have an automatic method of representing hierarchy.

Hierarchy and lists

List-orientated languages do allow the tree diagram structure to be represented simply. It is normal to use round brackets to "drop" to the next level in the hierarchy, as all keyboards have this character and it does actually mean something similar to us already. This leads us into defining lists – which are simply collections of words separated by spaces.

To show how this is done, we will use the standard round brackets to denote a list. Thus,

    (hello, how are you?)

is a list of 4 elements, each separated from the next by a space. The first element, or 'head' of this list is 'hello,'. Notice that the comma is part of the element as there is no space between it and the word 'hello'. The next three elements form the 'tail' of the list, and they constitute a smaller list. This is:

    (how are you?)

Again, brackets have been used to denote that this is a list.

Note that the order of the elements in the list is important, just as the order in which we use words is important. Each element may itself be a list. For instance,

    (hello, (is that you?) how are you?)

is a list of five elements, the second of which is a list of three elements, sometimes called a 'sublist'.

As you can see, lists are simply strings, where the spaces have some importance – they separate items called 'elements'. If an element is not a list, it is called an 'atom', as it is considered to be indivisible. Thus the list above contains four atoms, and a list of three atoms.

To see how to use lists, let us consider Figure 1.1 again. The first node contains two words, but they are associated together as the single entity:

    heavenly-body

We will, in general, use hyphens for the 'gluing together' of two words to form a single atom. This simply replaces the use of a space, which would cause this element to split into two atoms.

The first three elements of the tree in Figure 1.1 could be written as:

```
(heavenly-body (star-like planet-like))
```

This is a list of two elements – the element 'heavenly-body', and the (sub)list (star-like planet-like). The sublist is to be interpreted as being types of heavenly body, and hence on the next level down in the tree. Technically, the list above contains an atom and a list. The sublist also contains two elements, each of which is an atom.

In order to extend the above list to contain more of Figure 1.1, we simply change one of the atoms in the sublist above into a list. For instance, 'planet-like' is at the head of a further two atoms – 'planet' and 'moon'. Thus, 'planet-like' could be extended to being the following list:

```
(planet-like (planet moon))
```

This is still a single element, but is not an atom – it is now a list of two elements – an atom, and a sublist. If we extended the list onwards from the atom star-like too, the first seven elements of Figure 1.1 would then be:

```
(heavenly-body ((star-like (single-point galaxy-shaped))
                (planet-like (planet moon)))))
```

Thus, extending the tree is simply a matter of increasing the levels of brackets within the list.

As you can see, this very soon becomes a task of counting brackets, and the above is indented to make it easier to read (hopefully!). Note that more than one space is interpreted as being the same as a single space.

This new list is again a list of two elements but with 'heavenly-body' as the head. The second element is a list enclosed in brackets, and you should make sure you can identify these two separate elements in the above. This second element consists of two elements, each of which contains an atom and a list, and these elements are written in columns in the above to point them out.

The hierarchy of the data represented here is exactly as would be implied by brackets in the numeric part of a BASIC program. That is, the innermost brackets are at the lowest level, and the outermost brackets at the highest. Furthermore, we are sticking to two elements in each list above as the tree has just two branches at each node. By this means we have successfully represented an otherwise 2-dimensional tree diagram in a linear form which may be input from a keyboard. It is then up to our program, and the programming language to use and interpret this correctly. The process above is extended in the same way, until the whole of Figure 1.1 is stored in the list. Figure 1.4 shows a further stage in the process, and again it is set out in a special manner. However, when these objects are typed in, they are typed in a single line, without indenting. You should examine this figure in detail, and see how it ties up with Figure 1.1. Again, check that you can see how many sublists there are, and how many elements overall.

```
(heavenly-body((star-like  ((single-point ( . . . .))
                            (galaxy-shaped( . . . .))))
              (planet-like((planet(Earth not-Earth))
                           (moon   ( . . . . . . . ))))))))
```

Fig. 1.4   Hierarchy of heavenly bodies

The problem, of course, is that all this is quite difficult to analyse, and really needs a tree diagram to help you to understand and manipulate the structure. The difficulty arises from the fact that a 2-dimensional structure is being represented by a 1-dimensional object. It would be considerably easier if the tree data, with all the data pointers represented by the branches, could be encoded within simple two-element lists, all on the same level. This would save having to worry about how many levels of brackets were needed. Let us see what facilities would be required for this type of arrangement.

Association lists

Now that you have been introduced to lists and data trees, you can see how a really sophisticated list-processing language should treat these objects. Suppose we were simply to break the tree up into lots of triples of the form:

   `(planet-like (planet moon))`

Note that this is a list of two elements, the second of which is itself a list of two elements, but we will refer to it as a triple, here, for short.

The head of each such list simply contains the data at one of the nodes of the tree, and the tail of the list gives the data found at the ends of the two branches which emanate from it. Each of the pieces of data in the tail would be at the head of its own triple, and thus all the data in the tree could be encoded in triples. Figure 1.1 is contained in the following list:

```
( (heavenly-body (star-like planet-like))
  (star-like (single-point galaxy-shaped))
  (planet-like (planet moon))
  (planet (Earth not-Earth))
  (Earth)
  (not-Earth ( . . . ))
  (planet (. . . . ))
  (         (  .         )
            .
            .
  (         (  .         )
```

Notice how all the triples are on the same bracket level here.

The list is simply a collection of lists. Each one has a data node in its head, and an associated pair of data nodes in its tail. The connection throughout the tree is achieved by the fact that each atom in the tail will itself be the head of another triple somewhere else. There is no complexity of hierarchy, and the order in which the triples appear in the list is irrelevant, as long as they all appear. This means that more nodes and branches can be added to the list anywhere convenient – such as onto the end or the beginning. Extending the list is very simple.

A miraculous command

The next question is to decide upon the type of list-handling facility which would be useful for the use of this encoded database. For instance, it would be miraculous if there were a command which simply said 'find me the triple which has "planet" as its head'.

If such a command were to exist, the guessing game program would start off by asking for the triple with 'heavenly-body' in its head. The associated tail would provide two choices for the program to present to the user. He would choose one of them, and this choice would appear somewhere as the head of a triple in the database. Our 'miraculous' command would then be used to find this next triple, and thus the next two pieces of data. This would simply be repeated until a piece of data such as 'Earth' is reached. At this point, the triple-finding command would bring back a triple which had an empty tail. This would be taken as the signal that the process had come to an end.

To work this properly, a further set of commands is required. We need to be able to isolate the head and tail of a list separately. As each triple is found, we need to take the tail, and split that up into head and tail, and so on. In short, we need list analysis commands. We also need to be able to recognise the empty list when it arises.

It is easy to extend the above database tree to allow an arbitrary number of branches in the tree from a given point. Simply include more atoms in the tails of the 'triples'. The analysis functions for finding the head and tail can be applied over and over again to find any member of a list, no matter how long. For instance, the head of the tail of the tail of:

(A B C D)

is C – check that you agree!

Conclusion

To write BASIC procedures or subroutines to perform even the above list-processing commands is a complicated and time-consuming business. The result would also be quite slow, and to gain higher speed, the routines would have to be written in machine code – an even more cumbersome procedure.

This is the reason that a list-processing language such as LISP is used – all the facilities described above, including the very general 'find a triple' command, are available as direct commands in LISP. In fact, the facilities described so far only scratch the surface of the language. There are other facilities which LISP offers that are not necessarily confined to list-processing specifically, but allow greater subtlety and structuring of programs than can be achieved with many other languages.

There are many other applications for list-processing than those mentioned above. For example, list-processing is used for 'parsing' which is the intelligent analysis of natural language sentences. The human brain performs parsing continuously while understanding communication. One of the goals of AI is to perform this function automatically. Also, list-processing is used to aid the mathematician in proving theorems and manipulating algebraic expressions.

There are many more applications of LISP, and related languages, but the first task is to learn the language itself.

Summary

Intelligence is best assessed if communication is efficient, indeed communication is at the basis of our conception of intelligence. Communication is based upon lists of words – hence one good reason for having a computer language, such as LISP, which is list-orientated. *Expert systems* are another application of an intelligent activity. This depends upon a database, or knowledge base, which is a list of data – hence, again, the importance of list-processing.

Games may be played by considering *trees* of data, or trees of actions to be performed. A list-processing language will present internal facilities for manipulating trees without the explicit building and defining tasks for the tree structure itself. This saves time and energy, and allows the effort to go where it is needed – into the intelligent manipulation programs, rather than into the mechanical housekeeping tasks, as would be required within BASIC.

A *list* is a collection of items separated by spaces. Round brackets are usually used to confine a list. Lists may contain sublists as elements; the brackets give a certain hierarchy to the object, with the outer brackets being at the highest level – in some sense, very much as the brackets imply when in BASIC arithmetic expressions. Association lists are lists of sublists, each sublist having a head which is used as an index to the data in that sublist. This allows a complete tree of data to be stored, and added to at will with great ease.

Chapter Two
The Fundamentals of LISP

Introduction

This chapter will show you how to start using the standard LISP functions. It follows the normal computer language path of discussing data and variable types first, so that you can be clear about the types of object which the language acts upon, as well as the types of data it manipulates. The next task is to look at some of the typical simple constructs of the language, which are built in. These will be compared to similar BASIC keywords, and structures where possible, and it is assumed that you have some familiarity with typical standard functions and facilities. It is not easy to give anything but simple examples at this stage, and larger examples are left to the next chapter, where program writing in LISP is discussed. The present chapter effectively contains the 'nuts and bolts' of LISP, and little can be done until you have mastered the principles described below. You should try all the examples given, and if you have a computer, type them in at the same time. By doing this you will naturally build up an excellent grounding in the basic facilities of LISP. Answers to the numbered examples are given at the end of the chapter.

Data types – numbers and lists

LISP can be used to manipulate numbers, but it is generally very poor at this activity and will normally only allow integers to be used, and then only in the range −32768 to +32767. There are functions built in to add, subtract, multiply, and divide integers, but do not expect to be able to use the full gamut of BASIC floating point functions and calculations in LISP. If you do need this type of function, BASIC is normally a better bet.

The data type which is most commonly used in LISP programs is the 'list'. As explained in the last chapter, this is simply to be regarded as a string of items (characters, numbers, special characters, spaces as separators, etc.) containing sublists, and perhaps further levels of sublist below that. The normal notation for a list uses round brackets to enclose the members. The members of a list are separated from each other by 'separators' such as spaces, though other special characters can also be used. Examples of lists are:

```
(A B C D)        which has 4 members
(Hello There)    which has 2 members
(1 2 3 44 John)  which has 5 members
```

The important point about identifying the members of a list is that they are surrounded by spaces and/or brackets – no other symbol will do. For instance, the following lists may seem to have more members than they actually contain:

```
(Hello, how are-you?)
(1,234+68 is the-answer)
```

Both lists contain just 3 members. Commas, hyphens, etc. are part of the member they are attached to. In fact, the hyphen is a natural way of 'gluing' words together in normal writing, and above they are used to bind words together to form a single list member from two words. Any other character would have done, as the actual meaning of the symbol is not important here. You will have to check your own LISP version to see which non-alphabetic characters have special meaning, and steer clear of those.

A list may also have a single member, or no members at all. For instance,

```
(A)    or    (   A   )
```

has just one member. Note that the extra spaces are ignored, as they would be between two members in a list – more than one space is generally interpreted as a single space.

The list containing no members at all is called the empty list, and is written as:

```
()
```

A sublist is simply a list contained within another such as:

```
(A B (C D) E)
```

Here, the outer list contains four members, one of which is a list, or sublist, (C D) of two members.

Now that the concept of a list has been introduced, let us look closer at the members themselves, and introduce some important LISP words.

Atoms and identifiers

The lists above have been made up from members which were alphanumeric, and with the implication that the 'human' meaning of the words and numbers written there was irrelevant. Of course, in order to use the lists above, we must be able to regard the members of a list with some intelligence. To do this, we will look at the members themselves.

There are three member types in the above list – atoms, lists and identifiers. The words and numbers are called 'atoms', and the bracketed members are called lists (or sublists). The word 'atom' is essentially used to denote any item which is not a list. The word 'identifier' is used for those atoms which are not pure numbers. Identifiers may be thought of as atoms which form valid names, just as they do in BASIC. In fact, as in BASIC in general, most LISPs will insist that the first character of an identifier is a letter, and we shall assume this in the following.

In general, we will also not use non-alphanumeric characters in atoms apart from hyphens. If you need to do so, you should check your own LISP version carefully, by experiment.

To sum up these crucial definitions:

Atom: a single string of any type of character, with no spaces included. For example:

```
-17    Fred2-Smith   one2three    1256
```

List: a set of any number of atoms and/or lists separated by spaces and contained within round brackets. For example:

```
(12 3 7)       (A B (C D (E) F G))
```

Identifier: an atom which is not a pure number, and may be thus used as a variable or function name. For example:

```
Odd-number   X24   multiply-by-2
```

It is important to note that in LISP, case is important – lower-case letters are completely different from upper-case, as in natural language.

As a comparison with BASIC, it is tempting to think of lists as strings in BASIC. However, BASIC does not recognise the use of spaces between groups of characters within the string, nor does it have a concept of the sublist structure. The word 'string' will be used in the following from time to time, but will have no particular technical meaning; it will simply denote a collection of printable characters, and its use will be clear from the context.

The only other data types which we will meet are Boolean values and constants. These will be explained more fully when they arise, but a Boolean value is simply TRUE or FALSE, and a constant is a number or one of the Boolean values. In fact, LISP uses the notation T and NIL for TRUE and FALSE. Thus, NIL is a Boolean constant, and 67 is a numeric constant.

Variables

The reason for splitting off those atoms which are identifiers is similar to the reason for having identifiers in any other language. An identifier can be the name of a function or variable, which can take on any valid value within the language. In LISP, valid values are lists and atoms. The latter consists of numbers within the range defined above, and identifiers. In LISP, you do not need to distinguish separately between numeric and other types of variable.

Identifiers can thus be used to store the result of a numeric calculation, a string of letters and other characters, a list of any length and depth, or be used as the name of a function, as we shall see. In general, we will generally stick to identifiers which are readable, and thus describe their use. By this method, LISP code will be self-documenting.

We will see shortly how actually to assign values to variables, but the first task is to talk about the basics of a LISP session.

Starting with LISP

This book can be read without a computer to hand, if you simply wish to gain an idea of LISP. However, to become a LISP programmer, it is essential to try out the ideas and examples described here, and begin as early as possible to explore programming ideas of your own, no matter how simple.

The problem with describing the use of LISP is that different LISPs have different screen outputs, and even different internal functions. Of course, the majority will be the same or obviously similar, but the only way to see those differences is to refer to the manual with your LISP, and use it to see how to start.

Assuming that you have loaded the LISP interpreter into your computer, you will see some sort of prompt on the screen. Typing on the keyboard will enter characters as normal, with a moving cursor, and the usual deletion keys, etc.

EVALuation

In this book, we will use a prompt which looks like this:

EV:

There are good reasons for this, and the main one is that this prompt is short for 'EVAL' – a special function of LISP which attempts to evaluate anything it is given. In fact, much of the secret of LISP programming is to remember that *anything* you type in has a value, and this value is discovered by EVAL.

Thus the above prompt reminds us that the EVAL function is running all the time, and is constantly on the look-out for an object to evaluate. If you have just typed a random set of characters onto the screen, and ended with the usual ENTER or RETURN key on your keyboard, you should have an error message on the screen to tell you that EVAL cannot find a value for this object.

Note that error messages differ radically from machine to machine, and LISP to LISP, and you will have to read the relevant section of your manual for explanations of error messages.

Now try typing in a number after the EV: prompt, within the correct range. You will see that there is no problem in evaluating this object; the number itself will be displayed as the value. Numbers are objects which have numeric values – as one would expect. They are constants to which EVAL gives their obvious value.

The EV: prompt is actually asking for one of two types of object. It either wants a single atom which has been assigned a value, or a list containing a function which it can evaluate, as we shall see shortly. Any other object – for instance, two atoms typed in with spaces separating, and with no bounding brackets – will not be understood correctly. The actual reaction depends upon your dialect of LISP.

Assignment, standard LISP functions – SET and QUOTE

In BASIC, when we wish to write a program statement, we either use a line number – to ensure that the statement is remembered – or we type the statement directly for immediate execution. If the statement is an assignment, we either use LET, and an equals sign, or just the equals sign itself, in most BASICs. This performs the assignment immediately, and the value of the variable is retained for future use.

In comparison, LISP has no line numbers; it stores statements in a different form, as we shall see later. However, it can also perform an assignment statement immediately and recall the variable's value.

The function which performs assignment in BASIC is called LET. In LISP, the function is called SETQ. Assignment in LISP is referred to as 'binding'. Thus we say that a value is bound to a variable by the SETQ function. A variable which has no defined value is said to be unbound.

We will assume in the following that identifiers, used as names for the standard LISP functions, are all in upper-case, though you can define new functions in either. However, remember that an upper-case identifier is different from the same identifier with even one of its letters in lower-case.

SETQ cannot be typed in immediately after the prompt because EVAL would try to evaluate the identifier SETQ, rather than using SETQ as a function.

To see how functions are used in LISP, the following is an example of an assignment, using the function SETQ for binding the value 64 to the variable called Number:

EV: (SETQ Number 64)

As you can see, the function is used at the head of a list, with arguments following in the tail.

As usual, you must end each line with a RETURN or ENTER, as appropriate on your machine.

Try it, and you will see that EVAL has evaluated the list above to give the value 64. It will signify this to you by printing that value on the screen, perhaps with a message. This underlines the fact that EVAL's only job is to produce a value from the objects it is given. EVAL looks either for an atom, or a list. If it finds an atom, it simply prints out its value, if it has one. If it finds a list, as in this example, it looks for an atom at the head of the list. Here it finds the head atom SETQ, automatically assumes it is the identifier of a function name and looks for the definition of that function. SETQ's definition tells EVAL not to try to evaluate its first argument, Number, but to go straight to its second argument, evaluate it, and then store it in the variable 'Number'.

The purpose of the function SETQ is to store the value of its second argument in the identifier written as the first argument.

Following the above, it should now be clear to you that typing the atom Number after the prompt will display the value 64, because this is now its value. Try it.

As a further observation on the above, you can see that EVAL itself is a function which takes just one argument, either an atom, whose value it prints, or a list which it treats as a function in the manner described above. In general, if you give EVAL more than one argument, such as two atoms without bounding brackets, it disregards all but the first.

The above shows how to assign numeric values to a variable, but LISP is more concerned with using lists as values of variables, so that these lists can be manipulated and analysed.

To use a list as the value of a variable, it follows from the above that this list should appear as the second argument in a SETQ function. However, the list has to be written in a special way, as the following shows. Consider the example:

```
(SETQ X (This is a list))
```

You might imagine that this gives X the value:

```
(This is a list)
```

But, this is not the case – remember that one of EVAL's tasks was actually to evaluate the second argument of a SETQ list before applying SETQ. Thus, when EVAL goes to work on SETQ's second argument, it notices that it is a list, and EVAL tries to interpret the first member of the list as a function name, just as it did above. This can be useful, but here will produce an error, unless you have already defined a function called This.

As you can see, we need some way of telling EVAL whether the argument it is acting upon at any time is to be regarded literally as written, or whether its value is to be found.

The QUOTE function does this, and the following is the corrected argument for EVAL, which you can now type in:

```
(SETQ X (QUOTE (This is a list)))
```

As usual, EVAL finds the SETQ function at the beginning of its argument-list, and then looks at SETQ's second argument, which is the two-member list:

```
(QUOTE (This is a list))
```

Again, EVAL expects the first member to be a function and finds the QUOTE function, with a single argument. This is similar to the double quotes used in BASIC to signify that what follows is to be taken literally, and not evaluated. The QUOTEd list above thus has the value:

```
(This is a list)
```

This list is then bound to X by SETQ. If you type in X, you will see that it has worked. X now has a list as a value, just as it might have a number, or any other type of atom. Setting X to a given atom involves the same procedure. Again, it is essential that the given atom is taken literally, and not actually evaluated, unless it is a pure number such as 34 or −678.

To set X to the atom HELLO-THERE, for instance, we use QUOTE again, but this time its single argument is an atom, and does not require brackets:

```
(SETQ X (QUOTE HELLO-THERE))
```

This will set X to the atom HELLO-THERE. If you put brackets around this atom, it becomes a list with a single element. This may seem a small difference here, but it will be vital later.

QUOTE is used so often in LISP that there is an abbreviation for it. The single quote mark ' is used as follows to give the same effect as above:

```
(SETQ X '(This is a list))
```

and

```
(SETQ X 'HELLO-THERE)
```

This also saves on a set of brackets, which is even more worthwhile!

The use of the quote will be seen to be essential in distinguishing between literal objects, which are simply meant to be strings of characters, and the values of those objects.

As a simple example of the way in which QUOTE is used, try typing in the following examples:

```
'(HELLO THERE)
'HELLO-THERE
'X
```

You will see that all that is printed each time is whatever appears after the QUOTE – as long as you keep it to just one argument.

The SET function

You may have wondered about the fact that the EVAL function only evaluates the second argument of SETQ, and leaves the first alone. In fact, the Q on the end of this function is short for QUOTE, and is placed there specifically to make it clear to EVAL that the argument following is to be taken literally. There is an associated function called SET which does allow EVAL to act on both of its arguments before the assignment is performed. It is important that both arguments have a previously defined value, and that the first argument is not a constant such as 34, as this cannot be assigned a new value.

Thus, (SET X Y) will evaluate both X and Y. It then sets the object which is the *value* of X equal to Y's value. Note that X itself does not change, only the value of its value is altered. This is a little subtle, and is best seen by carefully following the example below.

First, consider the variable called NUM, which is set equal to the atom SIX using:

```
(SETQ NUM 'SIX)
```

If you type this in and then inspect the value of NUM by typing it in directly, you will see, as you should expect by now, that its value is SIX. SIX itself is undefined at this point, which you can check by typing it in. To give SIX some value, say the number 6, you could simply type in (SETQ SIX 6). However, there is another way which uses just SET, and the definition given above. The list to type in is:

```
(SET NUM 6)
```

It is tempting to imagine that the number 6 is stored in NUM by this command. However, SET allows both of its arguments to be evaluated, and when EVAL acts on NUM, it finds that its value is SIX, and it is this which is set to the number 6. Thus, the above function actually changes the value of SIX, and not that of NUM. If you now type SIX into the machine, you will see that its value is 6, and typing in NUM will show that its value, SIX, has remained unchanged. If you now type the above function list in again, but this time including a Q on the end of SET, or a ' in front of NUM (but not both), you will see that it is NUM which is changed this time, and SIX is left untouched.

Thus, you can either use SETQ or use SET and a QUOTE to assign a value to a variable. For instance, the following are the same:

```
(SETQ X 56)
(SET 'X 56)
```

In general, if there are two possible representations, as above, we will stick to the convention that SETQ is the only assignment function available, except in special circumstances where SET may be needed.

It should be mentioned here that *missing quotes are one of the most common causes of bugs in LISP programs*, and this particular difference in SET and SETQ can cause hidden value changes which may not show up until considerably further on in a program.

List-processing – heads and tails

As mentioned in the last chapter, in order to understand the structure of data storage, it is necessary to think of any list as having a 'head', which is simply the first element, and a 'tail', which is the rest of the list. In fact, any list may be thought of as being composed of just these two objects, and this provides a powerful method of analysing, bit by bit, any given list, no matter how complex. Let us consider some examples.

The list:

    (A B C D E F)

has the atom A as head, and list (B C D E F) as tail. The head of a list is not necessarily an atom. For instance:

    ((A B C) D E F)

has the list (A B C) as head, and (D E F) as tail.

This analysis can be carried on further. D is the head of (D E F), and (E F) the tail, and so on. This can be quite complex, and you should convince yourself that the tail of the tail of the head of ((A B C) D E F) is (C), as an example. Note that the tail of the type of list shown here is itself a list, not an atom, and thus the answer here is a *list* (C). However, there is a very simple type of list whose tail is an atom, as we shall see later in this chapter.

In the examples above, each list and sublist considered had both a head and a tail. However, what is the tail of the singleton list (A)? The head is the atom A, but the tail is the empty list. In fact, you should be able to see that every list has the empty list as its final tail. In LISP, the empty list is given a constant value: NIL – which is the same as the FALSE Boolean value.

Example 2.1

(a) Find the head of the tail of:

    (Hello, how are you?)

(b) Find the tail of the tail of the tail of:

    (I hate computers)

(c) Find the head of the tail of the tail of:

```
(A (B C) (D E) (F G (H)))
```

Head and tail functions – CAR and CDR

As you can see, analysing a complex list containing sublists can always be done by taking nested head and tail functions as shown above. In LISP, there are two functions for taking lists apart in this fashion. They are called, rather unmnemonically, CAR and CDR. They each take a single argument.

The CAR of a list gives its head, and the CDR its tail. To remember which is which, it may help to remember that the A in CAR is the head of the alphabet. They are used in the same way as all LISP functions – i.e. as the head of a list with arguments in its tail. Thus, if you type in:

```
(CAR '((A B) C))
```

EVAL will recognise that this is not an atom, and hence assume that the head of this list is a function name with argument: '((A B) C). EVAL then tries, as usual, to evaluate this argument, and finds the QUOTE to tell it that the value of this argument is the list literally appearing after the QUOTE. Thus it goes no further and passes the value:

```
((A B) C)
```

to the function CAR. This returns (A B), which is printed as the result.

This has been described in detail to give you a further example of the internal workings of LISP. Grasping this sequence of operations is crucial to the ability to program in LISP. You should read this explanation carefully, and be sure that you have the sequence set in your mind before continuing.

Remember that if the QUOTE had been omitted above, then EVAL would have tried to evaluate the list, and would have expected its head, (A B), to be a function name, with argument C. This would have led very quickly to an error. Again, you can see how important it is to use the QUOTE correctly.

CDR is used in a similar manner, as follows:

```
(CDR '((A B) C))
```

Check that you can find the result before typing this in.

If you need to set other variables to the head and tail of a list, SETQ is used as follows:

```
(SETQ Head (CAR '(A B C D)))
(SETQ Tail (CDR '(A B C D)))
```

These give Head the value A, and Tail the value (B C D). This gives a good example of nested functions. Any level of nesting is possible, and EVAL simply strikes through to the innermost brackets, or QUOTE, and starts evaluating from there outwards. Here, it strikes a QUOTE, and goes no further. CAR and CDR are evaluated by EVAL, and used as the second argument of SETQ. These are then stored in Head and Tail respectively. Once again, imagine for yourself what would happen if the QUOTE were left out.

To analyse a list further, CAR and CDR can be nested as many times as required. For instance, you should check for yourself that the atom B is the value of:

```
(SETQ X(CAR(CDR(CAR '((A B C)D E F)))))
```

Just look through for the innermost set of brackets, or the QUOTE, and work outwards writing down the intermediate stage values as you go – this is how LISP does it.

Note that for illustration the minimum number of spaces has been used. It is not a bad idea, in general, to put in a few more spaces than this to make the expression more readable, but you do not normally need them. Note that it is assumed that the QUOTE may not be used as a separator, and thus it must be preceded by a space, or it will become mixed up with CAR, and may then give the identifier CAR' which LISP will not understand.

This nesting of CAR and CDR can be performed more easily to a shallow depth using some extended forms of CAR and CDR which you will find most useful in simple analyses. If extra As and Ds are placed within the words CAR and CDR, these act as extra head and tail directives respectively. Thus, CAAR is the head of the head of a list, and CDDR is the tail of the tail. You can also mix these. For instance, CADR is the head of the tail of a list, reading from left to right. Similarly, CDAR is the tail of the head. Up to 3 letters can normally be placed between C and R, in any mix, in this type of word. Check your own LISP to be sure. As examples, check the following:

```
(CDDDR '((A B C) D E F G))   gives   (F G)
(CDDAR '((A B C) D E F G))   gives   (C)
(CDDDR '((A B C) D E))       gives   NIL
(CADDR '((A B C) D E))       gives   E
```

The third example shows what happens when the final tail is empty. The value of the empty set is the atom NIL, which is a special LISP constant. We will examine this value in more detail when we look at relations and conditions a little later. For now, you can confirm that this is the value of the empty list by typing in () to see the effect of EVAL on this object.

The analysis of a complex tree of data stored as nested sublists is rather difficult using individual nested CAR and CDR functions as can be seen from the above. In BASIC, we might use a loop to make these functions act on a list repetitively until the required level is reached. This is one way that LISP can perform the complete analysis, but there is also a more powerful way of using a function over and over again to achieve this result. This will be covered in the chapter on recursion later on in the book.

Example 2.2

(a) Rewrite your answers to Example 2.1 using nested CAR and CDR functions, and then using the multiple functions such as CADDR.

(b) Write out complete LISP expressions, containing the list:

(here is (a sublist))

which have the following values:

(i) the atom a
(ii) the list ((a sublist))
(iii) the list (a sublist)

You should then try typing them into your computer and see if you can find more than one answer to the questions.

(c) What characteristic does the argument of the CDAR function always have to have?

Data storage – CONS-cells

The most important data type in LISP is the list, and in order to understand some of the subtleties of the language in the following, it is useful to have a conception of the way in which such data is stored within the computer. A full description of the data storage method is beyond the scope of this book, but there is a useful representation of the storage method which will aid in unravelling some of the most important points. This also shows how LISP automatically stores tree structures without having to construct them explicitly as in BASIC.

Lists are ordered sets of atoms and sublists, and the storage must be effected so that no matter how long and complex the list, each member points to the memory location of the next wherever it may be stored. This type of 'linking' between members means that contiguous members do not need to be stored next to each other in memory. Thus, when a new piece is to be added, for instance, all that is needed is an adjustment to the pointers, and the list's integrity is guaranteed. Of course, a list handling system such as this would be reasonably complex to administer if the user had to take care of the pointers himself. This is one of LISP's main tasks, and the process is continuing in a completely transparent manner all the time.

To gain an appreciation of the storage method for lists, a special tree of box-like elements, called CONS-cells, is often used in LISP. Each box contains two pointers. These point, in general, to the CAR and the CDR of the list (see Figure 2.1).

Figure 2.1 also shows the CONS-cell diagram for the list (X). It illustrates the LISP definition of this single-element-list, or 'singleton' list. It has X as its CAR, and NIL, or the empty list, as its CDR. Each half of the cell points to CAR or CDR of the list. The second half points to NIL, and this is so

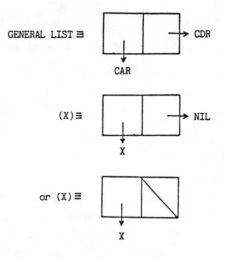

Fig. 2.1 CONS-cells

common that there is a shortened form where the second half has a diagonal drawn in it, as shown.

A larger list such as:

(A B C D)

has the representation shown in Figure 2.2. This shows how the pointer system works in memory. There is a CONS-cell for each member of the list,

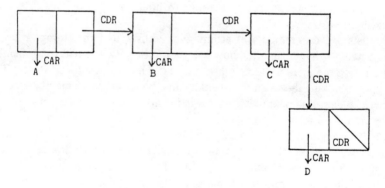

Fig. 2.2 CONS-cells for (A B C D)

the last one of which points to NIL. Notice that the first CONS-cell of the list points to the CAR of the list, and to a set of CONS-cells representing the CDR. The same is true throughout the diagram at each intermediate part of the representation.

A more complex list has a tree of CONS-cells. For instance, consider the list:

(A (B C) D (E F (G H)))

To see how this can be represented, note that it only has four members. Thus, there will be four CONS-cells at the top-most level, the last of which points to NIL. Some of these four CONS-cells will point to further lists, each

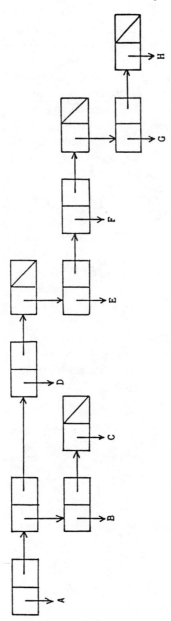

Fig. 2.3 More complex list

represented again by a number of CONS-cells equal to the number of elements, the last of which points to NIL. See if you can sort this out in Figure 2.3. You can see that the structure of LISP is very tree-like in its data storage.

Example 2.3

One of the uses of this type of diagram is to make the meaning of nests of CAR and CDR functions a little clearer. See if you can sort out the CDADR of this list from the diagram before reading on.

The clue is to start at the right-most function – CDR – then go to CAR, and finally to CDR. Also, note that this diagram is arranged so that each use of CDR goes to the right, and each use of CAR goes downwards. Simply use your hand to cover up the CAR pointed to by the first cell, which is A, and what is left is the CDR. Continue this process to find the answer. If you have a computer, you can check that you are right. If you do not have a computer, go back to the bracket representation of the list, and work it out again, before looking up the answer.

Many of the deeper ideas of LISP can be better understood using a CONS-cell representation. For instance, the concept of different lists which are lexically identical, i.e. contain the same characters. We will look at this next.

Consider the following two SETQ operations:

```
(SETQ X '(A B))
(SETQ Y '(A B))
```

The identifiers X and Y are bound to values which appear to be identical. However, Figure 2.4 shows the actual situation – X and Y point to different sets of memory locations, which happen to have the same ASCII codes stored there.

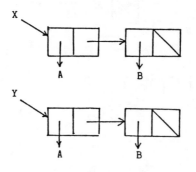

Fig. 2.4 The list (A B)

However, Figure 2.5 illustrates the following situation:

```
(SETQ X '(A B))
(SETQ Y X)
```

In this case, X and Y are bound to the same actual list. If anything is now done to X, say, its pointer will be removed from this list, and pointed towards the new value, and Y will remain bound to (A B). The importance of the distinction between Figures 2.4 and 2.5 comes when we look at Boolean relations shortly, and in particular the equality relation.

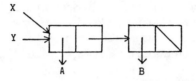

Fig. 2.5 X and Y equal to (A B)

CONS-cells may be constructed directly by LISP programs, and we shall see a construction function in the next section. In addition, a special notation is used to represent these cells, and this is described next.

Dotted pairs

The two-element list of Figure 2.5 can be stored more simply as shown in Figure 2.6. Here, there is no final binding to NIL, and only one CONS-cell is

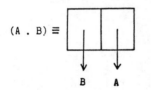

Fig. 2.6 A dotted pair (A . B)

used. This is a different structure from that shown in Figure 2.5. It is the simplest two-element list which can be formed in LISP, and it is written as

(A . B)

and called a 'dotted pair'. Note that it is a list, and hence must still have brackets. In many LISPs, it is necessary to put spaces before and after the dot, to prevent it from being mixed up with A and B. We will assume this here, though this is not universal, and you should experiment with your own LISP.

To see the difference between:

```
(A B) and (A . B)
```

consider the use of CAR and CDR. Figures 2.5 and 2.6 show that CAR of either gives the atom A, as this is pointed to by the left-hand side of the first or only CONS-cell in each case. According to the rules, the right-hand side points to the CDR in both cases, and this is where the difference lies. Figure 2.5 shows that the CDR of (A B) is the CONS-cell having B at its head, and NIL at its tail. Figure 2.1 shows that this is actually the list (B). However, Figure 2.6 shows that the CDR of (A . B) is the atom B. This is the only type list whose CDR is an atom and not a list. The difference between (A . B) and (A B) is important because the next section describes a function to construct lists, and it will either produce a normal list, or a dotted pair depending upon its arguments.

Before turning to list construction, it is important to see exactly what the 'dot' above generally represents. It can normally be considered as the pointer between CONS-cells. For instance, in Figure 2.5, the list (A B) shown can be written as:

```
(A . (B))
```

The dot is the pointer between the two CONS-cells. You should try typing this into your LISP, with a QUOTE, to see that it will print it out as:

```
(A B)
```

Similarly, larger lists can be represented using the dot notation. For instance, Figure 2.2 could be written as:

```
(A . (B . (C . (D))))
```

Also, just as Figure 2.6 is (A . B), so Figure 2.1 is the same as (X . NIL). You can actually type these dots into LISP, and EVAL will understand them as written above. For instance, try typing in:

```
'(Hello . (there . (George)))
```

and you will get the value:

```
(Hello there George)
```

as the result. This is the same as the dotted notation, but EVAL prefers to print the value in as simple a form as possible. Try some others for yourself. If you forget the QUOTE, an error will occur.

We now have a method of constructing any complexity of list from a set of values if we can use the dot as a function to join elements together. This is one method by which your programs can build up lists, and the next section shows how.

Example 2.4
Write down the dotted equivalents of:

(a) (A) – (use Figure 2.1 as a clue).
(b) ((A) B) – again, draw as a CONS-cell diagram first.
(c) (A (B C))
(d) ((A B) C)

You should try your answers on the computer, and see if you can produce more than one answer to these problems.

A further exercise, which will need a computer, is to rewrite the list represented by Figure 2.3 in dot form. This is quite complex, and you will find a computer useful to try out intermediate stages. Start by dotting together the top line of elements in the diagram, and then move down to the next layer, and so on.

As a further clue, the top line equals:

```
(A . ((B C) . (D . ((E F (G H)) . NIL))))
```

There are several answers, depending upon how many NILs you put in, and you will need your computer to check that you have found one.

CONS

CONS is a LISP function which simply dots its two arguments together. The result is found by considering the type of CONS-cell diagram which we have met so far. The following examples show how CONS acts:

```
(CONS 'A 'B)       gives (A . B)
(CONS 'A '(B C))   gives (A . (B C))   or   (A B C)
(CONS 'A NIL)      gives (A . NIL)     or   (A)
```

As you can see, CONS is simply the dot described above, and written in a form which constitutes a LISP function – i.e. it appears at the head of a list, with its (two) arguments in the tail.

CONS can be used, for instance, to add a further head to a given list. This is shown in the second case above where the head atom A is attached to the list (B C). This is a very powerful construction function, and acts in the opposite direction to CDR, which effectively strips the head off a list. In analysing a list, it is often very useful to strip off the head, and replace it with another, and perhaps do this throughout the list to each successive CDR in the list. We will see many examples of complex list manipulations in this book, and if you can keep the CONS-cell representation in your mind throughout, you will find these activities easy to grasp.

As you can see from the third case above, CONS can also be used to turn an atom into a single-element list. By this means, a list can be built up from scratch, using values from a set of variables. As an example of this, suppose that X, Y and Z have bound values:

```
X  =    heavenly-body
Y  =    star-like
Z  =    planet-like
```

These can be combined into the list:

```
(X (Y Z)) = (heavenly-body (star-like planet-like))
```

using CONS. The first step, until you are familiar with LISP, would be to draw the CONS-cell diagram, to tell you how to use CONS (see Figure 2.7).

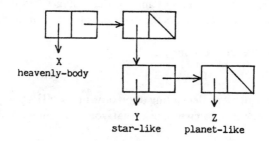

Fig. 2.7 CONS-cells for (heavenly-body (star-like planet-like))

To see how to use this diagram, let us start by building up (Y Z), which represents (star-like planet-like), which is the innermost list. The figure shows that Z is to be dotted to NIL, and this is the first operation. Thus:

```
(CONS Z NIL)
```

forms (planet-like). It is very important that you realise why the Z here is not quoted. The reason is that we actually want EVAL to evaluate it when it is reached in this function, so that it is the value, planet-like, which is turned into a list, not the letter Z itself. If Z were quoted, the list formed here would be (Z), which is not the value required.

The next operation, shown in Figure 2.7, is to dot Y onto this. Thus, two functions must be nested as follows:

```
(CONS Y (CONS Z NIL))
```

This gives (star-like planet-like). It does not store it anywhere; this is just the value of the function shown.

The next operation, according to the diagram, is to CONS this with NIL. Look at Figure 2.7 very carefully to see this – it comes from the second CONS-cell on the top line of cells, just as (CONS Z NIL) came from the second CONS-cell on the bottom line. The final operation, as you can see, is to dot in X. The whole nest of functions is as follows:

```
(CONS X (CONS (CONS Y (CONS Z NIL)) NIL))
```

Pick your way through this carefully before continuing. If you have trouble following it, write the above function out on a separate piece of paper, and isolate the two arguments which go with each use of the CONS function.

As you can see, the number of NILs in the function exactly ties up with the number of NILs drawn as diagonals in the figure. This is a useful quick check for a function of this sort. It also shows how important the NIL constant is in LISP. There are many more instances of this importance, and it is perhaps ironic that the most important list in LISP is actually the one which is completely empty! This is, in fact, a familiar situation in the field of mathematics, where such quantities as the empty set and zero occupy crucially important positions.

The above function certainly evaluates to the correct value, but in general this is not enough. We normally want to store the value formed in this way, and thus the above function would normally form the third argument of a SETQ expression.

The LIST function

In order to build up lists as above, there is a higher level function offered by LISP, which saves a lot of time. This simply creates a list of its arguments. It can take any number of arguments. For instance:

```
(LIST 'A 'B 'C)
```

has value (A B C). Note that if the QUOTEs are omitted the list will contain the values of A, B and C (if they exist) instead of these atoms literally.

To produce the list required in the last section, we could have written:

```
(LIST X (LIST Y Z))
```

This has the value:

```
(Heavenly-body (star-like planet-like))
```

and is much easier to write down. Observe again that since we wanted the actual values of X, Y and Z here, no QUOTEs were used, and EVAL evaluated them as it encountered them.

LIST is easier to use for this application than CONS, but there are cases where LIST is not quite powerful enough. For instance, suppose that the atom T has the value:

```
(there George)
```

and you want to add the atom Hello to the head of this list. You have to use CONS as follows:

```
(CONS 'Hello T)
```

which has value:

```
(Hello there George)
```

If you try:

```
(LIST 'Hello T)
```

this will produce:

```
(Hello (there George))
```

because it literally produces a list of the values of its arguments. Once again, the QUOTE before Hello prevents this word from being evaluated, while T is evaluated.

The topics introduced so far will have given you a reasonable familiarity with lists, and the inner workings of LISP. The next few sections introduce some more of the basic facilities of LISP before we move onto function definition, program construction and some examples. We will move through the following concepts quickly, because you should already be familiar with them from BASIC. However, if you are not, they are explained in enough detail for you to pick them up as you go along.

Example 2.5
(a) Use CONS to build up:

```
((A B) C)
```

using just the atoms A, B, C and NIL. Remember that CONS is used to add a head to a list, so start off by adding the head (A B) to the list (C).

(b) Use LIST instead of CONS in (a).

(c) Using CONS, write down an expression which would store the list (Hello Mary) in the variable SENTENCE given that the variable NAME has the list value (Mary) and GREETING the list value (Hello).

(d) Do the same as in (c) but using LIST.

Boolean relations and predicates

In BASIC, relations such as $>$ and $<$ are used to compare two quantities. This forms a test condition for use in such statements as :

```
IF  condition  THEN  action.
```

The condition has the Boolean value TRUE or FALSE, and the action occurs if the condition is TRUE. Also, in many BASIC dialects it is possible to write:

```
PRINT  (2 = 6 - 4)
```

This will not print the value 2, or the equation above literally; it will usually print the truth or otherwise of the equation. It may not actually print the

'Boolean' value TRUE or FALSE, but it will print out a number which is defined as one of these Boolean values. In LISP, the value of an assertion such as the one above is normally printed as T or NIL. These are the LISP constants which equal TRUE and FALSE respectively. Thus, if the above PRINT statement could be written in LISP, it would print the value T. Make sure that your version of LISP uses these actual identifiers for the values concerned.

T and NIL are constant values just like the numbers, and you can even use SETQ to set an identifier to T or NIL, and thus bind it to one of the Boolean values.

Just as BASIC has the relations:

$= < >$ etc.,

to provide methods of setting up conditions which have TRUE or FALSE values, so LISP has analogies to these relations.

In LISP, a conditional relation is referred to as a 'predicate', and some of the relations end in P to denote that they are predicates.

The relations available on most LISP packages are:

EQ GREATERP LESSP NULL ATOM LISTP NUMBERP ONEP ZEROP

There may be others on yours, and some of the above may even be missing. You should keep your LISP manual close to hand as you try out the examples in this book.

The relations above are used in the same way as all LISP functions. Each may only be used as the first item in a list, followed by arguments. The value which they return is either T or NIL, and nothing else. They are used, essentially, for testing, and are defined as follows.

EQ tests whether two objects are equal, and returns T or NIL accordingly. It takes two arguments only. Thus:

```
(EQ 2 2)
(EQ X 'heavenly-body)
```

All have the value T, or TRUE, if X is set as in the preceding examples. The following:

```
(EQ 2 4)
(EQ X 'Heavenly-body)
(EQ 'A '(A))
```

all have the value NIL. The first is obvious, the second is false because an upper-case H has been used, and the third compares the atom A with the list (A).

GREATERP and LESSP compare their first argument with the second, in the obvious way. The two arguments may only be numeric – these predicates do not apply to alphanumeric quantities, in most LISPs. Examples of their use are:

```
(GREATERP  6  2)      equivalent to  6 > 2 in BASIC
(LESSP 2 6)           equivalent to  2 < 6 in BASIC
```

Both have the value T. Also, if NUM1 has value 16, and NUM2 has value 35, the following values hold:

```
(LESSP NUM1 NUM2)     has value   T
(GREATERP NUM1 NUM2) has value   NIL
```

NULL tests for the value NIL, and takes a single argument. Thus, the following have value T:

```
(NULL ()  )
(NULL (CDR '(A)))
(NULL (CDDR (CONS X (CONS Y NIL))))
```

If the QUOTE had been omitted in the second example, EVAL would have blundered through trying to evaluate (A), and would have discovered that A was not a defined function. The QUOTE tells EVAL to take (A) literally.

The reason for the third example having a TRUE value is that the innermost CONS produces a list with a single member, which is star-like. The next CONS adds heavenly-body at the head of this list, and produces a list with two members. The double CDR finds the NIL which is dotted onto the end of the two-member list, and NULL tests this to see if it is NIL. This is just the sort of use to which predicates such as NULL are put, and you should examine this example carefully before continuing.

ATOM LISTP and NUMBERP are used to test for the type of a given object. They return the value T if the argument is an atom, a list or a number respectively, and return NIL otherwise. They take single arguments. Thus, the following have value T:

```
(LISTP (CONS 'A 'B))
(NUMBERP 34)
(ATOM X)
(ATOM 'X)
```

Remember, that before the function is applied, the argument is always evaluated – if it is QUOTEd then the value is the argument literally. The third example assumes that X is set as in the previous examples.

ONEP and ZEROP take single arguments, and simply test for the numeric values 1 and 0 respectively. They are useful while manipulating lists of binary numbers, for instance.

As we shall see shortly, these predicates are used in LISP's conditional statements, just as in the IF statement in BASIC. In the same way, there are Boolean operators, NOT, OR and AND, to allow the building up of larger, more complex predicates. These are used as follows:

OR takes any number of arguments, and evaluates them from left to right. As soon as it finds one which has value T, it returns the value T. If it finds none which are TRUE, it returns NIL.

AND is similar, but it only returns T if all of its arguments are TRUE.

NOT takes a single argument, and returns NIL if its argument evaluates to T, and vice versa.

Each is used as for all functions – the operator heads a list with the arguments in the tail.

The following examples show the use of these operators.

(i) `(OR (EQ 2 2) (EQ 2 4) (EQ X 'heavenly-body))`

The OR operator here has three predicates as arguments. The first compares 2 and 2, and has value T. This is far enough to see that the whole expression must return T, as at least one of OR's arguments is TRUE.

(ii) `(AND (EQ Y 'star-like) (OR (EQ 2 2) (EQ 2 4)))`

The AND here has two arguments. The first argument compares the value of Y, and the atom star-like. This is TRUE if set as for the previous examples above. The second argument is an OR predicate with two arguments, the first of which is TRUE, and hence the OR returns TRUE. This means that both of the AND's arguments have value T, and thus the AND returns T.

(iii) `(NOT (EQ 2 2))`

Here the NOT has an EQ predicate as argument, and the EQ is clearly TRUE. This means that the NOT returns NIL. A more complex example is:

`(NOT (OR (EQ 3 4)(EQ X 'heavenly-body)(EQ Y '(A B))))`

You should convince yourself that the value of this predicate is NIL, and try typing the expression into your machine.

As you can see, any test can be produced from the basic operators above. You can, for instance, produce the test for greater-than-or-equal from GREATERP and EQ. Thus:

`A >= B`

would be written in LISP as:

`(OR (EQ A B) (GREATERP A B))`

or as:

`(NOT (LESSP A B))`

which is somewhat neater.

Example 2.6

(a) Write out expressions for:

   (i) A $<>$ B
   (ii) A $<=$ B

(b) Construct an expression which would be T if X is NIL or if X is a list, but NIL otherwise.

(c) Construct an expression containing X which is T if the value of X is an identifier.

An important point should be made here regarding the construction of large and convoluted predicates. This does, of course, provide a powerful programming tool. However, one of the main tenets of structured programming is that one should keep the complexity to a minimum. LISP is a naturally structured language, and it is rarely necessary to use large and convoluted predicates in a properly constructed LISP program. It is generally better to split the expressions into smaller modules, for instance.

A further point should be made regarding EQ. If you are testing lists, you can find that even though two lists contain the same data, they are actually unequal. The EQ relation usually tests for exact equality, that is the two variables must point to the same list, as in Figure 2.5, for EQ to have the value T. The similarity of Figure 2.6 is not enough. For instance, if you type in the following;

```
(EQ '(A B) '(A B))
```

you will find, with most LISPs, that the value is NIL, despite the fact that the arguments appear equal. There is normally no such problem with atoms. Only lists have the CONS-cell structure whereby the same data can be stored at different places, and hence define different lists, as far as EQ is concerned.

There is a related predicate which is usually referred to as EQUAL, but may well not be implemented in your version of LISP. You can create it for yourself, and this will be done in Chapter 5. EQUAL tests for equality as for EQ, but includes the case where two lists are the same, but stored in different places. EQUAL is more useful for many list applications than EQ.

Arithmetic

Arithmetic in LISP is restricted to integers, and a few arithmetic functions. There are no BASIC-type floating point functions in most LISPs. The normal arithmetic functions available are:

```
PLUS   DIFFERENCE   TIMES   QUOTIENT   REMAINDER
```

There may be others, such as MINUS for changing the sign of a given number, and you should check your version of LISP to be sure. These functions are actually sufficient to build up any complexity of arithmetic functions required, but this is rare in LISP programs. The most common uses of arithmetic are for counting in loops, very much as one might use a loop counter in BASIC.

The functions work as follows. PLUS, DIFFERENCE and TIMES

generally take two arguments, and produce their sum, difference and product respectively. You should check your LISP, however, as it is possible that your version allows multiple arguments for some of the arithmetic functions. Acornsoft LISP does, for instance. We will assume two arguments here unless otherwise stated.

Examples of the use of these functions are:

```
(PLUS 3 67)           has value    70
(DIFFERENCE 18  38)   has value   -20
(TIMES  16  -5)       has value   -80
```

As usual, the function name appears as the head of a list with arguments in the tail.

QUOTIENT takes two arguments, and finds the division of the first argument by the second. It rounds off to give the nearest integer to zero if the division does not give an exact integer. Thus a positive quotient is truncated to the nearest integer below, and a negative quotient to the nearest integer above. This has the effect of keeping the remainder positive.

REMAINDER takes two arguments, and finds the positive remainder on applying QUOTIENT to the two arguments.

Examples of these two functions are:

```
(QUOTIENT 17 3)     has value   5
(QUOTIENT -17 3)    has value  -5
(REMAINDER 17 3)    has value   2
(REMAINDER -17 3)   has value   2
```

Both REMAINDER and QUOTIENT must have non-zero second arguments.

The arithmetic functions can be nested as far as required, just as in BASIC, and used as part of predicates.

However, it is fair to add that to perform complex calculations, with speed, LISP is not the best language to choose. It is possible to define functions in LISP in a completely intrinsic manner, which make them indistinguishable from the standard LISP functions. However, if the basic arithmetic functions above were used to produce a full scientific floating point package, this package would be slower in its operation than that of a good BASIC package.

Summary

Data types – numbers are integers from -32768 to $+32767$, Boolean values are T and NIL, and lists are elements separated by spaces and enclosed in round brackets.

Atoms are non-lists. They include numbers and identifiers.

Indentifiers are alphanumeric strings, without spaces. In some LISPs identifiers have to start with a letter – check yours.

Constants and *variables*: In LISP, all the pure numbers, plus T and NIL are special constants. All other atoms may be variables, and may take on any value, including atoms and lists.

EV: is used as the system prompt in this book.

EVAL is a single argument function which is running all the time. When EVAL comes across an atom, it tries to find its value, unless it is quoted. If it comes across a list, it will expect the head of that list to be a function name, followed by arguments, which may also be evaluated, if unquoted.

Functions are named by identifiers which appear at the head of a list, with arguments in the tail.

SETQ is used by LISP as the equivalent of LET in BASIC. It takes two arguments, only evaluates the second, and sets the first equal to the value of the second.

QUOTE – or single quotation mark for short – implies that what follows is to be taken literally, and not evaluated.

SET is the same as SETQ except that it evaluates its first argument, and sets the value of its first argument, which should be an identifier, to the value of the second.

CAR is a function which takes a single list as its argument, and returns the head of that list, which may itself be a list.

CDR is a function which takes a list as argument, and returns the tail. It always produces a list as its value.

CAAR, CADR etc. are multiple-use functions of CAR and CDR, up to a maximum of three operations, usually.

CONS is a function which 'dots' two objects together. If the first is an atom, and the second a list, it produces a new list with the given atom as its head and the given list as its tail. Two atoms as arguments give a dotted pair as its value.

CONS-cell is a primitive storage structure of LISP which gives it its linked-list structure, suitable for storing trees of data.

Singleton is a list with a single member which may itself be an atom or a list.

LIST is a function which takes any number and type of arguments, and returns a list containing those arguments, evaluated if the arguments are not QUOTEd.

A predicate is an expression in LISP which has the value T or NIL. There are several predicate functions available depending upon your LISP. They include:

EQ which gives T if its two arguments are exactly equal.

GREATERP which gives T if its first argument is greater than its second, and only takes numeric arguments.

LESSP – as for GREATERP, but less-than instead.

NULL returns T if its single argument has value NIL.

ATOM, LISTP, NUMBERP, ZEROP, ONEP each returns T if the single argument is an atom, list, number, value 0 or value 1 respectively.

AND and *OR* are used to build up larger predicates, and each takes an arbitrary number of arguments. AND returns T if all arguments are T, OR returns T if any one of its arguments is T.

NOT returns T if its single argument is NIL, and vice versa.

PLUS, DIFFERENCE, TIMES, QUOTIENT and *REMAINDER* are the arithmetic functions which take two numeric arguments. QUOTIENT rounds off towards zero, usually – check your LISP.

Solutions to problems

Example 2.1:
(a) how (b) NIL (c) (D E)

Example 2.2
(a)
```
(CAR (CDR '(Hello, how are you?)))
or (CADR '(Hello, how are you?))
```

```
(CDR (CDR (CDR '(I hate computers))))
or (CDDDR '(I hate computers))
```

```
(CAR (CDR (CDR '(A (B C) (D E) (F G (H)))))))
or (CADDR '(A (B C) (D E) (F G (H))))
```
   If you forgot the QUOTEs, give yourself a black mark!

(b)
(i) `(CAR (CADDR '(here is (a sublist))))`
(ii) `(CDDR '(here is (a sublist)))`
In this example, the second application of CDR produces a singleton list which has a list as its single member – hence the double brackets. Taking the CAR of this then strips off the outer set of brackets, as in the next example.
(iii) `(CADDR '(here is (a sublist)))`

(c) As CDAR is the tail of a head, that head must be list, or CDAR cannot work on it, and it will give an error. Thus CDAR's argument must always have a list as a head.

Example 2.3
The answer is (C). Remember that a singleton list such as this is represented as a CONS cell with one half pointing to C, and the other half to NIL.

Example 2.4
(a) `(A . NIL)`
(b) `((A) . (B))` or `((A . NIL) . (B . NIL))`

(c) (A . ((B C))) or (A . ((B . (C))))
(d) ((A . (B)) . (C))

Example 2.5
(a) (CONS (CONS 'A (CONS 'B NIL)) (CONS 'C NIL))
(b) (LIST (LIST 'A 'B) 'C)
(c) (SETQ SENTENCE (CONS (CAR GREETING) NAME))
(d) (SETQ SENTENCE (LIST (CAR GREETING) (CAR NAME)))

Example 2.6
(a)
(i) (NOT (EQ A B))
(ii) (NOT (GREATERP A B)) is the neat solution

(b)
(NOT X) (LISTP X)) is the neatest solution, but there are always other possibilities for this type of question.

(c)
(AND (ATOM X) (NOT (NUMBERP X)))

Chapter Three
Functions, Conditionals and Loops

Introduction

This chapter will indicate a number of comparisons between BASIC and LISP, and you should be able to see where LISP's advantages lie.

In BASIC, line numbers are used to store program statements to allow them to be edited, and the program RUN at a later date. In LISP, there are no line numbers. Instead, programs and routines are stored as function definitions. To write a long program, you will generally split it up into a number of functions and define these separately. Once a function is defined, it can be used as an internal part of the LISP package itself, and is indistinguishable from the standard functions, apart from being slower. This method of writing programs tends to force you to split large tasks into smaller ones, which is no bad thing in programming.

This chapter uses the standard functions of the last chapter to show you how to construct your own routines, store programs, and explore some examples. Conditional functions are introduced to show you equivalents of the BASIC IF statement, and loops are also described. By this means, all the normal BASIC type activities can be performed, but in a different and novel form which you will find very well suited to a more human way of producing computer programs.

Solving problems

When we have a problem to work out in our everyday life, we rarely sit down and write out a set of operations in minute detail to solve it. We are more intuitive and generally descriptive in our methods of solving problems, and this is the reason why we actually have to learn the process of programming when we first meet a completely logical machine such as a computer. It is not natural for us to consider a minutely detailed recipe for solving a problem. In programming, we are more likely to be able to think of what the program does rather than the logical steps used to achieve the aim.

This approach to programming causes great inefficiencies in program writing. For a typical BASIC program, most people will simply start writing code, and generally work out the inputs and outputs as they go along. Even the general philosophy of the program, and what it will eventually do are often hazy until the programming is under way.

BASIC, and similar languages, are all involved in providing recipes or lists of imperative steps for solving a problem. For instance, to double a number in general, a BASIC program may look like this:

```
10    INPUT "Please type your number";X
20    Y=X*2
30    PRINT X;" Doubled is: ";Y
```

This is a set of steps which includes a recipe of exactly where to store the number input from the keyboard, how to double that number and store it somewhere else, and finally how to output the finished product to the screen. How would you now double a number? You would have to type in RUN, and follow instructions – hardly very descriptive of actually doubling a number. It would be more descriptive of the task if you could simply type it in as:

DOUBLE 34 PLEASE

One of the goals of AI is to allow this very human method of input to be accepted. LISP is actually constructed to allow a similar type of input as standard. In LISP, when you want to write a program to double a number, for instance, the first thing to think of is how the program will be used, i.e. how the human will actually double the number. As you should know by now, in LISP you would write something like:

(DOUBLE 34)

Only the brackets distinguish it from normal natural language text. You can even write:

(DOUBLE 34 Please Sir)

Functions are usually defined to ignore more arguments than are needed, and the polite additions above are thus ignominiously ignored by the computer! But, you can put them in if you wish.

If you were to write:

(Please DOUBLE 34 for me, old boy)

the computer would be unimpressed, and signal an error. Can you give the technical reason for this before reading on?

The only problem with this last form of the use of DOUBLE is that the EVAL function will have trouble in finding a well-defined function in the head of the above list.

The next step in the process of producing the doubling program is to define the actual doubling process itself. This is simple, and is explained in the next section. You can see, however, that a LISP programming task starts with the way in which the program will be used, by considering an identifier for a function, and then attacks the problem of performing the actions.

In BASIC, you will often become bogged down in the problem of how to produce nice-looking screens, how to store the intermediate variables, and how to print out the final result neatly. These tasks usually lead one to forget the main task of the program, and thus the actual actions are lost within the peripheral activities.

A better approach, of course, would be to define fully the inputs and outputs as a completely separate exercise, and then split the main task into small modules, and program all these parts separately. This is perfectly possible in BASIC, or any other language, and is part of the basis of structured programming. In LISP, however, you will find that you have little choice. Structuring is a natural and automatic part of LISP programming. Also, you will find that the standard printing facilities of LISP will often be quite sufficient for output, and little in the way of special printing routines will be required. Certainly, the standard facilities are sufficient to develop your programs initially, and you can neaten them up later if you wish. Input is also more natural in LISP, as we shall see shortly.

To sum up, you will find that more time and emphasis is placed on the main programming tasks than the peripherals in LISP.

Function definition - DEFUN

Let us have a look at defining a simple function such as DOUBLE. This function is to take just one numeric argument, and return double the given number. Once defined, as mentioned above, it would be used as follows:

(DOUBLE 45)

which would have the value 90. It would evaluate its argument before actually doubling.

To define this function, the standard LISP function DEFUN is used. As with all LISP functions, it is placed at the head of a list containing its arguments. Any number of arguments may be used, but the first two are always the new function's name and a list of its arguments. The other arguments of DEFUN provide the function definition. This looks like:

(DEFUN function-name (list of arguments) body of function)

The body of the function may be a large list of expressions using other standard and user-defined functions. These may use the given arguments, or any other variables which may have been defined before the function call. By this means, actions are taken in the body of the function, and the very last one performed just before the function is exited, gives the value which is returned by the function itself.

For instance, the function DOUBLE is formally defined by:

```
(DEFUN  DOUBLE  (X)
       (TIMES  2  X)))
```

To see this, use the general definition of DEFUN given above to match with this pattern, and see which parts do what.

When the function is used, as in:

```
(DOUBLE  24)
```

the value of the argument, 24, is passed on to X for use within the funtion body. The LISP interpreter simply replaces X by this value, and then applies the above definition. EVAL simply ploughs through the definition of DOUBLE, and returns the value of the last expression evaluated as the value of the function. This is the TIMES function here, and thus its value, 48, is returned as the actual value of the list given above with DOUBLE in its head.

X is said to be a dummy variable, as the user does not type in the letter X when the function is used. It is also called a 'local' variable because X can be in use elsewhere, and its value is carefully stored and then restored again after its use in DOUBLE. The value of X produced within the function body is always lost.

You should type this function definition in for yourself, and experiment with it. You do not actually have to type the body of the function in on a separate line. With so many spaces, in fact, it is quicker not to do so. However, we shall do so here as far as possible, as it helps to display the larger functions. If you copy this, be careful to use only returns and spaces. If you use TAB, for instance, you may find this gives an error which is rather difficult to sort out.

DOUBLE is now an internal function of LISP, and does not need to be separately defined for each programming use. It will be slower than the same complexity of standard LISP function, because standard functions are written in machine code You can do the same if your LISP package allows machine code to be linked in. Another difference, of course, is that you can adjust the definition of DOUBLE if you wish.

In fact, this is your first LISP program! Up until this point everything typed in was transient, and could not be recovered for future use. DOUBLE is stored, and forms part of the system. A LISP program, therefore, simply consists of a number of functions. A large program has a single function definition as its highest command, which consists of many smaller functions, in the body of its definition, each defined separately elsewhere. For instance, we can write a program to play chess as follows:

```
(DEFUN chess ()
      (SET-BOARD)
```

```
(ASK-NAMES)
(CHOOSE-COLOURS)
(PLAY-GAME) )
```

The first task in a LISP program is to choose a name for the function which will be typed at the head of a list after EV: in the usual way. The function is then defined as above, and starts by giving the function name, followed by a pair of brackets which are meant to contain the arguments. In this case, there are no arguments, and the argument list is empty. Then follows the complete chess program.

Simple, isn't it! It makes you wonder why they have so much trouble writing chess programs. Of course, there is the little detail of some function definitions for SET-BOARD, ASK-NAMES, etc.

The first three functions above are straightforward, and simply set up the screen display, ask for the players' names, and allocate colours to the players. The next function, PLAY-GAME, however, is the crunch. You actually have to program this function to play chess. When you have done so, in all its complexity, you will be able to play chess by typing in:

```
(Chess)
```

EVAL will then work its way down the function definition, evaluating as it goes, and will play chess with you.

In fact, all EVAL is doing here is trying to find a value for (Chess), and in so doing it has, incidentally, to work through all the expressions in the body of the function, and this happens to look to us as if it is playing chess. However, EVAL's final act, at the end of the game, will be to print up a value for (Chess), which is simply the value of the last expression evaluated. It is normal to make this a PRINT statement, or its equivalent, and hence end on a simple message of some kind. But, make no mistake, this last thing printed, as far as LISP is concerned, is the value of (Chess).

The main point about programming in LISP is that it should be thought of as a 'top-down' exercise which starts with the 'look' of the final function which will be used, and splits it into other modules which you can worry about later.

In LISP, you will often find yourself defining routines which are stored, and using these in immediate, or transient, routines. For instance, type in the following example:

```
(SETQ X 3)
(DOUBLE X)
```

This should give the value 6. Note, however, that even though the activities of DOUBLE are stored as part of a LISP program, the short routine here is forgotten as soon as it is used. You can store it, if you wish, by typing in:

```
(DEFUN DOUBLE-3 ()
    (SETQ X 3)
    (DOUBLE X) )
```

To use this function, type in:

```
(DOUBLE-3)
```

EVAL will look inside this list and evaluate the function it finds to give the number 6. This is hardly a very good example of a function as it is rather too specific, but you should be able to see the point that storage is a matter of defining a function if needed.

We will look at some further examples of LISP programs after the conditional function has been defined in the next section.

Example 3.1
(a)   Define a function called ADD3 which adds 3 to a number given as its argument.

(b)   Define a function called THREE which always returns the number 3; it takes no arguments.

(c)   Define a function called TRIADD which adds three numbers given as its arguments.

(d)   Define a function called CADDDR which returns the CAR of the CDDDR of a list – it takes a single argument.

(e)   Give a single example of the use of each of the four functions defined above. If you have a computer, try typing these in. What happens if you forget to include the brackets around the function on your LISP? Try it.

The conditional - COND

Every computer language, from machine code to BASIC, needs a conditional form of some kind to allow the program to make decisions. The conditional function in LISP is called COND, and its general use is, of course, at the head of a list containing arguments. COND may take any number of arguments, each of which is a list with a predicate (with value T or NIL) at its head, and an expression to be evaluated in its tail. We shall call these *predicate pairs* here. Thus, the general form of the COND function is:

```
(COND (predicate expression)
      (predicate expression)
      ( .                    )
      ( .                    )
      ( .                    ) )
```

Only one of these predicate pairs is fully evaluated. It is the one with the first TRUE predicate at its head. The final evaluation of the expression part of this predicate pair gives the value of the COND itself. Once again, remember that everything has a value in LISP.

As an example of this process, try typing in the following:

```
(COND (NIL  45)
      (T    60)
      (T    30)  )
```

(You can type this on one line if you wish)

EVAL starts at the head of this list, recognises COND, and moves to the head of the first sublist. Its head evaluates to NIL, and hence this sublist is abandoned. The head of the second sublist, however, has value TRUE, and the following expression, 60, is evaluated, and the COND finishes there – the next sublist is ignored. Thus, the COND list above has value 60.

Program evaluation rules

As emphasised above, it is absolutely vital to remember, through thick and thin, that anything you type after EV: has a value, for which EVAL is searching. This is somewhat alien to a BASIC programmer; when he RUNs a program, it does not have a value, it gives values to other things, or performs an action. In LISP, EV: is simply looking for a value. Thus, above, it is looking for a value for the COND list itself. In other words, as far as LISP is concerned the actual COND list represents a number or other constant, and the whole list could even be used in a numeric function. For instance, try typing in the following:

```
(TIMES (COND (T 45)(NIL 60)) 2)
```

Look first at the COND list; it has two predicates, and the first is TRUE. This gives the COND list itself the numeric value 45. The outer function, TIMES, then uses this value as its first argument, and 2 as its second argument. The result is 90, which the machine will print on the screen.

The value of a COND list might not be numeric, and care should be taken not to try to use it in a numeric function, as above, unless it definitely has a numeric value. The following examples have non-numeric values.

Example 3.2

Write down the values, or the possible values, of the following expressions:

(a) ```(COND (NIL 45) (NIL 60))```

(b) ```(COND ((EQ X 4) 'X-IS-4)
         (T 'X-IS-NOT-4))```

(c) Construct a COND list which will print out THIS-IS-AN-ATOM or

THIS-IS-A-LIST depending upon whether the value of a given object, X, is an atom or a list respectively. Remember that a QUOTEd identifier is evaluated to the identifier itself.

How would you store this COND list for future use?

Use of COND

As you can see, the COND construction in LISP is equivalent to an arbitrarily nested IF THEN ELSE function.

The expression following a predicate in a COND list can be a sequence of several evaluations, and only the last one will be returned. However, all the others will be performed, and this can be seen in the following example:

```
(COND (T (SETQ X 3) (SETQ Y 4)))
```

This COND has a predicate which has a TRUE head, and two lists in its tail, each with a SETQ. Both of the SETQs will be performed, but only the second will be returned as the value of the COND. Thus, if you type in the above, the final number to be printed by EVAL will be 4. However, if you inspect X, by typing it in directly, you will see that it has been set to 3. Thus, any number of actions can be performed after the first TRUE predicate in the COND list.

Storage

Once you have defined a new function, you can use it anywhere, and it effectively becomes internal until you switch the computer off. In order to transfer functions from one LISP session to another, the whole present state of the system can usually be stored. Your manual will tell you how to do this on your system. A typical method is simply to type in something like:

```
(SAVE 'file-name)
```

If you are using a cassette, you will have to switch it on first. A disk will be much faster, of course, and the files will be more accessible. LOAD is usually used to retrieve the data.

All that is stored is the list of function definitions, and any variable values. When LOAD is used, exactly as for SAVE above, the computer should revert to exactly the state it was in before saving the file. Again, it is in this type of area that different systems will act differently, and it is up to you to check this in your LISP manual. Some LISPs allow you to LOAD particular function definitions on their own.

You should also find that there is some file handling with your LISP, and this usually uses functions such as OPEN, CLOSE, WRITE, READ and so on.

An example function

It is difficult to give really useful examples at this stage, until you have more of LISP's facilities at your disposal, but the following example will help you to practise the features described so far. The problem in this example will be solved in two different ways to practise two different LISP programming techniques.

The problem is to define a function called TRI-SORT which sorts three numbers into ascending order.

In order to define the function, we must consider the intermediate tasks. The normal method is to check the first two numbers, and if they are the wrong way around, swop them, and write down the three numbers in the new order. Then look at the second and third, and again swop them if they are wrong. The final task is to look at the first two numbers again, and swop if necessary. You should try sorting three numbers in this way before continuing, to see how it works.

There are two ways to consider the definition of TRI-SORT, and the one chosen is dependent upon the method of presentation of the three numbers to be sorted.

If the numbers are to be given as values of three variables X, Y and Z, say, then we can assume that these variables are to remain in alphabetical order. It is the values which are to be swopped around until the order of the values is the same as that of the variables. A BASIC type of routine would be used to adjust the values of X, Y and Z until correct.

If the numbers are be given as a list stored in a variable L, say, then list manipulation functions could be used. In this case, there are no variables given containing the values.

We will consider these two solution methods separately, starting with the former.

Sorting the values of X, Y and Z

A BASIC program would use $>$ to check the values of the variables, and then use LET to reassign the values until the variables had the correct ascending values. We can do this in LISP too.

The following function acts on X, Y and Z, taken in order, and sorts their values into ascending order. It works by keeping the variables in alphabetic order, and changing their values.

```
(DEFUN TRI-SORT ()
  (COND ((GREATERP X Y)  (SETQ A X) (SETQ X Y) (SETQ Y A)))
  (COND ((GREATERP Y Z)  (SETQ A Y) (SETQ Y Z) (SETQ Z A)))
  (COND ((GREATERP X Y)  (SETQ A X) (SETQ X Y) (SETQ Y A))))
```

This function has no local variables, it assumes that X, Y and Z have been set previously, and returns their values sorted as required. There are three expressions in the body of the definition. Each is a COND with just one predicate pair. Remember that the expression part of each pair is only evaluated if the predicate has a TRUE value. The predicate in each pair checks the order of two of the variables' values, and the associated expression swops the values if they are in the wrong order. Note that one COND would not have been sufficient in this function, as only (at most) one of its predicate expressions is ever evaluated – the others are ignored.

The value of a function is that of the last expression evaluated in the body of the function. Here, either no swops are performed, in which case the function returns NIL, or a swop is performed, and a SETQ is the last expression evaluated. The returned value of this function is thus of no particular use. The function is simply used to act upon the values of X, Y and Z.

To use this function, X, Y and Z have to be set using a previous function, or some SETQ expressions used directly from the keyboard. The function then simply adjusts the values of X, Y and Z, and these values have then to be printed specifically by the user, if they are to be displayed.

This is very awkward. A better function would use three numbers given as arguments, and return the numbers in a list sorted into ascending order as the value of the function itself. This can be arranged by giving TRI-SORT some local variables, and returning these variables as a list in ascending order. The amended TRI-SORT would look like this:

```
(DEFUN TRI-SORT (X Y Z)
  (COND ((GREATERP X Y) (SETQ A X)(SETQ X Y)(SETQ Y A)))
  (COND ((GREATERP Y Z) (SETQ A Y)(SETQ Y Z)(SETQ Z A)))
  (COND ((GREATERP X Y) (SETQ A X)(SETQ X Y)(SETQ Y A)))
  (LIST X Y Z))
```

This can now be typed in, and experimented with. To use the function, type in the following:

```
(TRI-SORT 3 2 1)
```

The function will actually return the list (1 2 3) as its value, because the last expression evaluated in the function is the LIST function. If you try all this out, and then look at the values of X, Y and Z, you will see that their values have been untouched by the function. If they were undefined before TRI-SORT was used, they will be so afterwards. However, the value of A will have been changed; it is not a local variable as it is not declared specifically in the argument list of the DEFUN.

A further refinement on this function would be to define a function called SWOPIF, which would swop two numbers if they were in the wrong order. This might give a new version of TRI-SORT of the form:

```
(DEFUN TRI-SORT (X Y Z)
  (SWOPIF X Y)
  (SWOPIF Y Z)
  (SWOPIF X Y)
  (LIST X Y Z))
```

This is a better LISP program, as it contains the essence of the TRI-SORT function, but leaves the details of the SWOPIF part for later. However, it causes a problem, and brings us to one of the most important points about local and global variables. How do you write SWOPIF to ensure that the variables it uses are not entirely local to SWOPIF? Somehow we have to make SWOPIF act to change the values of any two variables it is given.

To see where the problem lies, suppose we were to define SWOPIF as follows:

```
(DEFUN SWOPIF (H J)
 (COND ((GREATERP H J) (SETQ K H)(SETQ H J)(SETQ J K))))
```

This certainly checks the two numbers H and J, and swops their values if H is greater than J, but H and J are local variables, and their new swopped values are lost when the function is finished. Furthermore, SWOPIF only returns the value of the last evaluation performed, which is just the last SETQ function, and is of no particular use. How do we make the function act on X and Y, say, and actually perform the swop?

You could use only variables which are non-local to the function. For instance, define SWOPIF as:

```
(DEFUN SWOPIF ()
 (COND ((GREATERP H J)(SETQ K H)(SETQ H J)(SETQ J K))))
```

The problem is that the function has to be called up using H and J specifically. Thus, to swop the values of X and Y, for instance, H and J have to be set to X and Y first. SWOPIF is then called up, which acts on H and J, and then X and Y have to be set to H and J. The whole process is far too cumbersome.

Another solution is actually to pass the atoms X and Y to SWOPIF, and make SWOPIF act on their values. To do this, SWOPIF has to be called up using:

```
(SWOPIF 'X 'Y)
```

or

```
(SWOPIF 'Y 'Z)
```

so that X, Y and Z are passed and acted upon literally. Unfortunately, while all this gives a useful illustration of the problems of local variables, it is still the wrong way to perform a swop, or indeed a sort in LISP. We are still using BASIC ideas, and the correct course is to return to the beginning of the definition of the sort function, and rewrite it in a form which is more applicable to LISP.

A LISP sort function

To perform a sort in LISP, we should be using list manipulation functions, instead of worrying about where to store the variables being sorted.

If the function TRI-SORT were always to act on a list of three numbers, we could isolate the first, second and third numbers using CAR and CDR. The swops would then be performed, and the actual list itself operated upon to give the final answer. A definition of TRI-SORT using lists would have a single argument which would be the given list of three numbers. It would be used as follows:

```
(TRI-SORT '(3 2 1))
```

or

```
(TRI-SORT L) if L had been set to (3 2 1).
```

The returned value of the function would be the list:

```
(1 2 3)
```

To see how to do this, you will have to recall from Chapter 2 how to use CAR, CDR, and all the multiple versions of these functions. In particular, you will have to check that you understand the following:

```
(CAR (3 2 1))    = 3
(CADR (3 2 1))   = 2
(CADDR (3 2 1))  = 1
```

If L is the list being operated upon, the top line of Figure 3.1 sketches the above as a diagram of CONS cells. If the first two members of L are in descending order, the first task is to swop them. This is shown diagrammatically in Figure 3.1. To swop two members of the list, we do not store one of them in an intermediate variable and use SETQ functions. All that is necessary is to construct a new list using functions such as LIST or

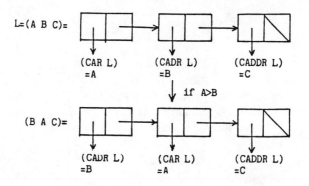

Fig. 3.1 Sorting three numbers

CONS with the two members swopped. For instance, to swop the first two members of a given list L, following the second line of Figure 3.1, we would use:

```
(LIST (CADR L) (CAR L) (CADDR L))
```

Thus, for instance, if you set L to (3 2 1) using:

(SETQ L '(3 2 1))   (remember to use QUOTE)

and type in the above function, the new value will be (2 3 1). This is considerably neater than the previous method of swopping, as well as being more direct – it acts on the list itself, rather than requiring intermediate storage. The value returned is immediately useful.

The swop of Figure 3.1 is only to be performed if the first two members are in the wrong order, and this would be written as:

```
(COND ((GREATERP (CAR L) (CADR L))
       (LIST (CADR L) (CAR L) (CADDR L)) ))
```

Here the LIST has been placed after a predicate in a COND list. The LIST is only performed if the first two elements of L are in the wrong order. The next problem is to use this to alter L itself, as well as performing the other swops if necessary. This gives a larger program than the last one for TRI-SORT, but one which is entirely list-orientated. The complete program is as follows:

```
(DEFUN TRI-SORT (L)
    (COND ((GREATERP (CAR L) (CADR L))
           (SETQ L (LIST (CADR L) (CAR L) (CADDR L)))))
    (COND ((GREATERP (CADR L) (CADDR L))
           (SETQ L (LIST (CAR L) (CADDR L) (CADR L)))))
    (COND ((GREATERP (CAR L) (CADR L))
           (SETQ L (LIST (CADR L) (CAR L) (CADDR L)))))
    L)
```

To understand this program, notice that it is composed of three possible swops. The indentations are used to help you to pick your way through the program. L is the given list, and the last line of the program ensures that there is a value given to the function if all the GREATERPs are FALSE, and none of the SETQs performed.

Using this function is easy, both from the keyboard, and from other functions, if required.

To use it from the keyboard, type in:

```
(TRI-SORT '(67 4 90))
```

This will return the list (4 67 90) as its value. Incidentally, this is a common place to miss out the QUOTE. If you find strange errors are signalled when you type in a value for a function literally from the keyboard, then this is a likely cause.

If the function is to be used from another function, it would be called up as:

```
(TRI-SORT K)
```

where K, from the outer function, has been given a value which is a 3-number list. When EVAL acts on this, it evaluates the argument K first, and then applies the definition of TRI-SORT. Note that K itself is left untouched by this function. If you want to change K, you will have to use:

```
(SETQ K (TRI-SORT K))
```

A useful exercise is to rewrite TRI-SORT to produce the list in descending order instead.

Example 3.3
Define a function, REPEATP, which checks for any repetition of the members of a list of three atoms. It should return T if there are two or more equal atoms in the list, and NIL otherwise.

Other types of function

The above introduces the use of the DEFUN function to give simple LISP functions with a constant number of arguments, each of which is evaluated when the function is called up. However, there is often a need to be able to define functions which do not evaluate their arguments, and which may have an arbitrary number of arguments. For instance, SETQ, and QUOTE do not evaluate their arguments – you do not have to use a quotation mark on the arguments of such functions. Also, functions such as TIMES can take as many arguments as you like. TIMES will simply multiply all these arguments together.

These extra facilities all exist in LISP, and we will return to these more advanced concepts, with some examples later on in the book. For now, the above is sufficient, and the last part of this chapter describes the last major structure which any programming language has to offer – i.e. loops. However, first we will take a short excursion into input and output in LISP, in order to increase the scope of the examples which can be given.

Input and output

There are two primary I/O functions in LISP. Again, these differ considerably from dialect to dialect, but we will only need the most primitive functions here, and you should find them available on your LISP. When you are fully conversant with the language, you can neaten up the I/O of your programs for yourself.

PRINT is used to print the value of an atom or expression, and READ is used to input a value from the keyboard. PRINT is not needed so often in very simple programs, as LISP prints the latest value on the screen automatically.

READ allows your programs to interact with the user, very much as INPUT does in BASIC.

PRINT is used as in the following examples:

```
(PRINT 34)   prints 34
(PRINT 'HELLO)   prints HELLO
(PRINT '(1 2 3))  prints (1 2 3)
(PRINT Z)   prints the value of Z
(PRINT (SETQ A '(Hello There)))  prints (Hello There)
```

Its value is always the value it prints, and so after performing the actual PRINT to the screen, EVAL will then perform its own print of the value, and thus the above will actually show the printed value twice on the screen. PRINT is useful for printing out intermediate results, or messages, during the processing of a program.

In the simplest case, READ is used without an argument to halt the program, and await a single input from the user. Depending upon the LISP you are using, READ with an argument may be used to read data from a disk file. We will assume that READ does not evaluate its argument. In the simple use of READ, the following is a typical use:

```
(READ)
```

This will cause the computer to stop, probably with a cursor on the screen. It is waiting for you to type in a single item. This single item is then returned as the value of (READ), and may be used by another function accordingly.

As an example of this function, the following is a function to print out the head of the tail of any list typed in:

```
(CADR (READ))
```

It is important to remember that this will give an error if anything but a list of two or more members is typed in. Also, no QUOTE is required as the READ function does not evaluate the input – simply type in a list with round brackets, and containing more than one member. We will see further examples of PRINT and READ shortly, but before reading on, try using these functions for yourself on your own machine, if you have one. Do not bother, for the moment, with the more sophisticated PRINT and READ functions your LISP may have. The ones above are quite sufficient for now.

Loops

In order to perform a repetitive sequence of operations, it is always essential in a programming language to be able to define loops. This is where different LISP dialects differ quite considerably – you will have to check your own manual fairly carefully. We will assume for this book that there is a function called LOOP which simply evaluates a sequence of expressions placed as arguments to the LOOP function. This is a common looping method, and all LISPs should have something similar. The typical general form of the LOOP function is as follows:

```
(LOOP   sequence of expressions)
```

When EVAL sees this, it simply evaluates the sequence of expressions over and over again, either forever, or until an error is found. Your LISP will probably allow you to break out of such a loop by using an UNTIL or a WHILE function. These functions take predicate pair expressions exactly as COND, and are used as follows:

```
(LOOP   (UNTIL   predicate expressions)
        (    sequence    of    expressions   ) )
```
or:

```
(LOOP   (WHILE   predicate expressions)
        ( sequence of expressions ))
```

The first of these loops continues until the predicate in the first argument of UNTIL is TRUE, and the second while the predicate in the first argument of WHILE is TRUE. The LOOP then ends, and only then does it evaluate the expressions in the subsequent arguments of UNTIL and WHILE. Notice that in each case the UNTIL or WHILE is the last function to be evaluated at the loop's end. Thus, in a similar way to COND, the last one of the expressions following the predicate controls the single functional value of the LOOP which is returned. We will see this in some examples below.

Note that the expression part of the predicate pair is optional. If you simply want to break out of the loop, and are not worried about LOOP's returned value, leave out the expression part.

In general, it is not necessary for a programming language to supply both UNTIL and WHILE, and just one of these will do – each is the logical complement of the other. Thus (WHILE X) is the same as (UNTIL (NOT X)), and vice versa. In the programs given in this book we will simply adopt the convention that only UNTIL is available. You may have to consult your LISP manual and discover the loop exit functions you have, and rewrite the programs here as required. It may even be that LOOP is produced in a completely different way in your LISP. There is always some way of performing loops, and once you know how, it is a very straightforward matter to convert accordingly.

Some examples

As an example of an infinite loop, try typing in the following after you have read the section of your manual which tells you how to break out of an infinite loop (ESC is a common key to hit under these circumstances):

```
(LOOP (PRINT (READ)))
```

This simply takes in any keyboard input you type, and prints it. A very neat method of allowing a break from this loop is to use:

```
(LOOP (UNTIL (EQ (PRINT (READ)) 'END)))
```

Here, the LOOP list contains just one expression to evaluate. It is an UNTIL with a single argument – the predicate EQ which compares an expression with the atom END. The UNTIL has no further expression arguments to be evaluated if the predicate is TRUE, and the loop simply finishes.

The UNTIL is evaluated with each loop, and this causes the EQ to be evaluated, along with everything within it. Thus the PRINT and READ are evaluated with each pass of the loop. As long as you do not type in END, whatever you do type is faithfully printed. When END is typed, the EQ becomes TRUE, and the loop comes to an end. At this point, the value of the LOOP is simply the last expression to have been evaluated. This is the EQ here, and its value T is printed as LOOP's final value.

Looping is useful for any program which requires an arbitrary number of actions to be performed. For instance, let us define a function which simply adds up all the numbers typed in, and finishes when END is typed in. We will define the function so that it returns the accumulated value.

The function will be called ADDUP, and it does not need any arguments. The definition is:

```
(DEFUN ADDUP ()
    (SETQ Y 0)
    (LOOP (UNTIL (EQ (SETQ X (READ)) 'END))
        (SETQ Y (PLUS Y X)))
    Y )
```

This is very like a BASIC routine. It sets out the actions to be performed in sequence. Y is set to 0 at the start, as Y is to be used to accumulate the total. The next expression is a loop which takes in numbers from the keyboard, and adds them to Y. It is important that only numbers are typed in, except for the atom END. The READ is once again confined to the UNTIL function. When END is typed in, the loop finishes. At this point, the loop is exited, and the expression following the LOOP list is evaluated. This is the atom Y, which has the accumulated total stored in it. As this is the last thing evaluated, it is the value of the function ADDUP. Note that the UNTIL or WHILE can be put anywhere in the loop; no exit will occur until one of these causes an exit, or there is an error.

After ADDUP has been used, the values of X and Y are retained at their last values, because they are not declared in an argument list as local variables. Can you see what the value of X must be after the function has been used – assuming that no error was signalled?

Let us now look at some list examples, which are nearer to the type of application for which LISP was developed.

Some simple list examples

We will now look at some examples which act on lists using loops.

Have a go at drawing a flowchart, and writing the program for each of the following examples, before looking up the answers which are given at the end of the chapter. If you need a clue, look at the flowcharts given in the answers before writing your function definitions.

Example 3.4
We can already find the first member of a list, using CAR, but how can we find the last member? Define a new function called LAST which finds this member. The clue is that the definition of the last member is the one which is followed by NIL in the list. You will have to use CAR and CDR in this example.

Example 3.5
Define a function called REVERSE which reverses the order of the members of a given list. The clue is that CONS will have to be used successively on the CAR of sublists of L.

Example 3.6
Use REVERSE to give another definition of LAST.

Example 3.7
We can easily add a new member to the head of a list, using CONS. How would you use the above to define a new function CONSR which adds a new member to the end of a given list? How would you then use CONSR to add the members:

    Peter Smith

to the list:

    (My name is)

Example 3.8
So far, we have no way of appending a list onto the end of another list. If we use CONS, or LIST, all we can produce is a list containing the given lists as sublists. For instance:

    (LIST '(1 2 3) '(4 5 6))

gives:

    ((1 2 3) (4 5 6))

The LISP function which gives (1 2 3 4 5 6) from these two lists is called APPEND. Not all LISPs actually have this function as standard, and it is not abnormal for the user to have to construct the function for himself.

When we look at recursion, we will see a very neat method of defining APPEND. For now, use the above functions to define APPEND.

Example 3.9
In AI, a typical task is to analyse a sentence. This requires, among other things, matching of the words in the sentence with a vocabulary. The sentence is treated as a list, and its members as atoms to be matched with a given vocabulary word. The sentence would normally be stored as the list value of a variable.

As a variation of this, define a function called MEMP which takes an atom, representing a word, as its single argument. It takes in the sentence as a list from the keyboard, and returns T if the given word is found in the sentence, and NIL otherwise. The whole list is typed in with surrounding brackets, and no QUOTE, before the matching is done.

A harder example
Sorting is a very basic function required in all forms of data processing. There are several levels of task required. At the start of this chapter, you were shown how to sort three numbers into ascending order.

The first task in an extended version of this sort method is to be able to 'bubble' the largest number in a list of arbitrary length to the end of the list. The next task is to perform the same thing again on the whole list, perhaps with the end member left out to save time. This task repeated will give a sorted list. You now have enough sub-functions available to be able to do this, and your final problem is to provide a sort function called SORT which takes a list of numbers and returns the list sorted into ascending order. You should then check that you can do the same for descending order.

There is no solution given in this chapter for the problem, but we will return to it in the final chapter, where the technique of recursion will be used. If you can solve it – which is not too complex, in fact – you will be able to understand the rest of the book with ease.

Conclusion

It is usual for books on LISP to imply that recursion is the only way to solve problems in list processing and AI. While it is true that recursion is a most powerful and useful tool, it is not true to say that it is completely essential. The aim of this chapter is to show you how you can do many things in LISP with just loops. However, another important lesson is that recursion is better for these tasks – a point which will only become clear to you when you have read Chapter 5. In addition, a full understanding of recursion can only come from a familiarity with normal looping and all the other elements of the language so far. It is thus essential for you to work through the exercises and examples as you read through the book.

Before we proceed to recursion, the next chapter fills in some more about list processing, and how to use some very powerful functions provided by LISP to store and manipulate data and knowledge bases for applications such as expert systems.

Summary

Program storage. In LISP, programs are stored as definitions of functions. Once a function is defined, using DEFUN, it is available as an internal facility of LISP, as if it had been a standard function.

DEFUN takes three types of argument. Its first argument is a function name, which is an identifier. The second argument is a list of arguments for the function to be defined. The rest of the arguments are expressions which are to be evaluated as the body of the function. The single value of the function is simply the last value of the last item evaluated in the body of the function. The list of arguments in DEFUN's second argument contains entirely local variables, whose value is left completely unchanged by the function.

COND is the equivalent of BASIC's IF THEN ELSE structure. COND takes an arbitrary number of arguments, each of which is a list. The head of each such list contains a predicate, and the subsequent items within the list are expressions which are only evaluated if the predicate has value T. COND will only evaluate the list following the first T predicate. The COND finishes there, and all other arguments are ignored. The very last thing evaluated gives its value to the whole COND expression itself upon exit from the COND.

SAVE and *LOAD* should allow you to store and retrieve your LISP program. This type of activity is entirely dependent upon your particular LISP, and you should consult your manual. Incidentally, these functions are used at the head of a list containing their arguments, just as all other LISP functions. They also have values, which are normally simply the name of the file being stored or retrieved.

PRINT evaluates its argument, and prints the value to the screen. The value of the PRINT list is the object printed.

READ has value equal to the next keyboard entry terminated with a RETURN.

LOOP takes an arbitrary number of arguments, and simply evaluates them over and over again until the loop is terminated by some function, or by an error. The LOOP list has value equal to the last item evaluated before exit.

UNTIL and *WHILE*. These functions take a predicate as their first argument. If the predicate is T, their subsequent arguments are evaluated, and the loop terminated. Processing then continues with the expression immediately following the LOOP list. UNTIL and WHILE return a value which is the final object evaluated within their list. This is thus the value of the LOOP upon termination.

Solutions to problems

Example 3.1

(a) This function takes a single argument, adds 3, and as long as this is the final operation performed by the function, it is returned as the function's value:

```
(DEFUN   ADD3  (X)
   (PLUS 3 X)  )
```

(b) This function differs from the last in that it has no argument, it simply returns the number 3 every time. The last evaluation in the function must produce 3:

```
(DEFUN THREE  ()
     3 )
```

(c) This uses the PLUS function. However, PLUS can only take two arguments, so you will have to use it to add the numbers two at a time:

```
(DEFUN TRIADD (X Y Z)
   (PLUS X (PLUS Y Z))  )
```

As you can see, the outer PLUS will be the last function evaluated, and hence its value will be returned as the function's value.

(d) This simply adds a further CAR function after the use of CDDDR on a list or variable with a list value:

```
(DEFUN CADDDR  (X)
   (CAR (CDDDR X)))
```

(e) To use these functions, simply type them in as heads of a list, with arguments in the tail. Examples of their use are:

```
(ADD3 5)   which has value 8
(THREE)    which has the value 3
(TRIADD 3 4 5) which has the value 12
(CADDDR '(A B C D)) which has the value D
```

If you now try typing one of the function names without brackets, you should be returned a list of the defining expressions of the function. The exact form of this list depends upon your copy of LISP, but its form will be a little difficult to understand until we look more deeply into functions in a later chapter. Meanwhile, notice that you can inspect a function definition in this manner. Try typing in:

```
TRIADD
```

to see the effect.

As a final note, try typing SETQ or some other LISP function without brackets. You will see that the definition of these functions is not presented; they are all defined by machine code routines, and you cannot inspect their definitions.

Example 3.2

(a) None of the predicates in the predicate pairs in TRUE, and the COND returns the value NIL.

(b) This is an example of the use of one of the conditional expressions from the last chapter. If the EQ expression is TRUE, then the COND returns: X-IS-4. If not, the next predicate list has a head which is always TRUE, and the COND will then return: X-IS-NOT-4. Note that if the QUOTE is omitted, EVAL tries to evaluate these messages instead.

(c) The following achieves the required action:

```
(COND ((ATOM X) 'THIS-IS-AN-ATOM)
      ((LISTP X) 'THIS-IS-A-LIST))
```

Whichever predicate has the value T will allow the following expression to be evaluated in that predicate pair. This automatically prints the required message, as a by-product of EVAL acting on the expression. This is generally a good way of producing messages quickly and simply in LISP.

If you type in the above, after having SETQ X to some value, you can test the function. However, you will have to type it in completely each time you wish to use it. To store it, you must use it as a function definition, and hence give it a name by which you can call it up any time you wish. The following defines it as the function OBJTYPE:

```
(DEFUN OBJTYPE (X)
   (COND ((ATOM X) 'THIS-IS-AN-ATOM)
         ((LISTP X) 'THIS-IS-A-LIST)))
```

Example 3.3

The function simply checks the first member against the other two, and then checks the second member against the third. The EQ function will be used, which is adequate because of the restriction to list members which are atoms:

```
(DEFUN REPEATP (L)
    (COND ((EQ (CAR L) (CADR L)) T)
          ((EQ (CAR L) (CADDR L)) T)
          ((EQ (CADR L) (CADDR L)) T)
          (T NIL) ) )
```

Note that the function contains four predicate pairs in the COND list. The first three check for repeats as explained above. If one of them is successful, the T (a LISP constant) in the expression following the predicate is evaluated, to T, and is the returned value of the function. Otherwise, the fourth predicate, which is simply the constant T, is TRUE, and its expression is the constant NIL which is returned as the function value.

Example 3.4

As given above, the definition of the last member is the one which is

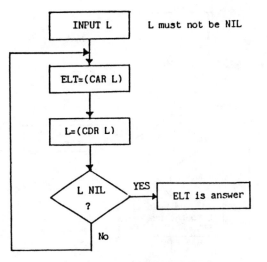

Fig. 3.2 Flowchart for LAST

followed by NIL in the list. This gives a good test for the last member within a loop. Figure 3.2 shows a flowchart for finding the last element of a list of arbitrary length.

The given list is L. Its first element is stored in the variable ELT (short for element), and L is set to its own CDR. This effectively strips the head off L, and stores it in ELT. If L had only one element, then it now has none, and its last (and only) element is stored in ELT. Thus, when the decision box in Figure 3.2 is reached, L is NIL, and ELT is the final answer. If L had more elements to start with, the process repeats, shortening L as it goes, until it only has one element. The process then repeats a final time, making L empty, and the value of ELT is the final answer.

The flowchart can be coded in several ways, but there will only be minor differences between them. The following is a possible version:

```
(DEFUN LAST (L)
    (LOOP   (SETQ ELT (CAR L))
            (SETQ L (CDR L))
            (UNTIL (NULL L) ELT)))
```

Here, the decision box is replaced by UNTIL which exits when L is NIL as required. However, the UNTIL function contains a further argument, ELT, which will be evaluated as the last action before the exit occurs. This ensures that the LAST function returns the actual last element as its value.

The UNTIL is placed last in the body of the function, as is the decision box in the flowchart, to ensure that the other expressions are evaluated at least once. Note that this means that L must be a non-empty list, or the list manipulation functions will give an error. However, just out of interest, you can use the list (NIL) if you wish. This is not empty – it is just the singleton list containing the constant atom NIL.

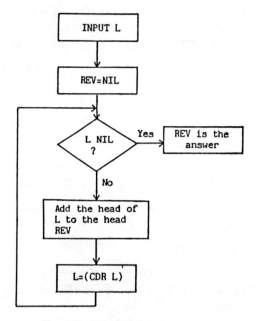

Fig. 3.3 Flowchart for REVERSE

If you can, try running this function, with as varied a test list as possible. Try putting in sublists, and sublists of sublists, particularly in the last position. You will find that it copes perfectly well, no matter how complex the list.

Example 3.5

Figure 3.3 shows a flowchart for this function. An intermediate variable REV is used to store the list which is gradually built up to being the reverse of L. REV starts off as NIL, so that it will not be undefined if it is required at the very start of the flowchart.

The decision box contains a check to see if L is NIL. In most LISPs, NIL and the empty list () are the same – you might check yours if the program below gives an error at this point.

If L is the empty list, then NIL is the correct answer to the REVERSE function, and thus REV already contains the answer for this situation. If L has several members, the rest of the loop will be used. The main part of the loop starts by taking the head off L, and CONSing it to REV, which places it at the head of REV, with NIL following, initially. If you remember the CONS-cells introduced earlier, you will know that REV is now a singleton list. L is then reduced by removing its head. Assuming that L still has some members in it, the process is repeated again, and the head of L is once again added to the head of REV. If you think this through, you will see that the first two members of L now appear, in reverse order, in REV. This continues until L is empty, at which point REV has the reverse of L stored in it.

Coding this function follows the flowchart exactly. The first expression is a SETQ for REV. The following is the final definition:

```
(DEFUN  REVERSE  (L)
    (SETQ REV NIL)
    (LOOP (UNTIL (NULL L) REV)
          (SETQ REV (CONS (CAR L) REV))
          (SETQ L (CDR L))))
```

Again, the loop exit occurs via UNTIL which evaluates REV as its final act, to pass the value of REV to the function.

Incidentally, it is worth noting that nowhere in our examples have we used variables with the same name as the function itself. For instance, here, we have used REV, not REVERSE. The reason is that the use of REVERSE as a variable will redefine it globally, as it is not a local variable. This redefinition, as a value, will remove its definition as a function. Similarly, the LISP standard functions should never be used as global variables. In fact, it safer never to use a standard LISP word as a variable in any situation, as some very strange errors can be produced in this way.

Example 3.6
To find the last member of a list, we could simply reverse the order of the list, using REVERSE, and take the CAR of this new list. Thus, a new version of LAST could be defined as:

```
(DEFUN LAST (L)
    (CAR (REVERSE L)))
```

Neat – eh?

Example 3.7
The idea of this function is to use REVERSE to reverse the given list, add the new member to the head of this, and reverse it again. We will define CONSR to have two arguments, with the list to be extended in the first, and the new member in the second. As a series of actions, with intermediate storage, CONSR would be defined as:

```
(DEFUN CONSR (L NEW-MEMBER)
    (SETQ L (REVERSE L))
    (SETQ L (CONS NEW-MEMBER L))
    (REVERSE L))
```

But, there is a neater way to say the same thing, by nesting functions. This would be:

```
(DEFUN CONSR (L NEW-MEMBER)
    (REVERSE (CONS (NEW-MEMBER (REVERSE L)))))
```

You should read this from the innermost bracket outwards, and visualise the intermediate processes. It is true that this is rather more difficult to read, but it saves space and time. Now try the specific example given in the problem.

To solve this example of adding Peter Smith to the given list, CONSR must be used twice in a row. You cannot simply write:

```
(CONSR '(My name is) 'Peter 'Smith)
```

for instance, as CONSR only takes two arguments. This will simply add Peter, and ignore the extra argument. It must be written as:

```
(CONSR (CONSR '(My name is) 'Peter) 'Smith)
```

Did you do this correctly but forget the QUOTEs? It would not be surprising. You will find that this is still the most common source of errors.

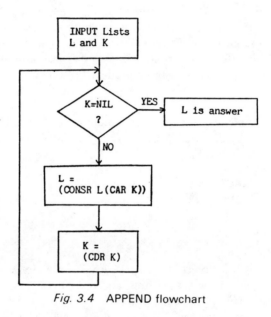

Fig. 3.4 APPEND flowchart

Example 3.8
Figure 3.4 shows the flowchart for APPEND. You should be able to follow and code this for yourself by now. The following gives a coding of this flowchart.

```
(DEFUN APPEND (L K)
       (LOOP (UNTIL (NULL K) L)
             (SETQ L (CONSR L (CAR K)))
             (SETQ K (CDR K))))
```

You must be sure to use only lists as arguments for APPEND, otherwise it will give an error. Try this function out for yourself, with as many different types of list as you can think of. You will see in the chapter on recursion that this definition for APPEND is longer than is necessary. However, it works perfectly well, and shows how the basic functions of LISP can be built up into quite general routines.

Example 3.9

The main part of this function uses CAR and READ. The idea is to reduce the given list from its head downwards, checking for the given atom as it goes. The program is as follows:

```
(DEFUN MEMP (MEMBER)
    (SETQ L (READ))
    (LOOP (UNTIL (NULL L) NIL)
          (UNTIL (EQ MEMBER (CAR L)))
          (SETQ L (CDR L))))
```

This gives a good example of two possible exits from a program. As the loop proceeds, it may be that the atom being searched for is not present, and L is reduced to NIL by stripping off its head over and over again. Then the first UNTIL will terminate the loop, with NIL as its final value. If, on the other hand, the atom is found in the input list, then the second UNTIL will succeed, and the value of that final predicate, which must be T, will be returned by the function.

To use this program, simply type in something like:

```
(MEMP 'hello)
```

The screen will show a cursor, and will be waiting for you to input a sentence list. Your input must be between round brackets, and the answer will be T or NIL. For instance, if you type in:

```
(Yes, hello, this is Peter)
```

The function will return NIL, because hello is followed by a comma. If you leave out the comma, the function will return T instead.

The reason for restricting the list to a list of atoms was to prevent any possible sublists containing the matching atom. This would not have been recognised by MEMP – can you see why? Also, the matching element is restricted to being an atom, rather than a list, because of the use of EQ in the function. Two lists are only EQ if they have identical memory location pointers. See the relevant section of the last chapter.

Chapter Four
Further List Processing

Introduction

The first three chapters of this book introduced the main parts of LISP, in comparison with BASIC where possible. You should be clear by now that LISP has the same general facilities as all other computer languages, but is presented in a different way from most.

This chapter introduces concepts which are largely unavailable in the procedural 'imperative' type languages such as BASIC. These concepts and facilities are specifically aimed at allowing the easy manipulation of lists and databases.

Chapter 1 introduced some of the concepts which will be described in this chapter, and you should refresh your memory on association lists in particular before proceeding.

The first part of this chapter introduces two main high-level facilities available in LISP, before examples and some further standard LISP functions are given.

Association lists - ASSOC

You should recall from Chapter 1 that one of the main problems in dealing with databases is to provide the data structures. Once the data is stored correctly, the programming is often quite straightforward. One of the most important data structures in existence is the tree structure. Chapter 1 gave an example of a tree of data based around a guessing game involving heavenly bodies. We will continue with this example in this section, to show how to set up and retrieve information using association lists.

The main point about association lists is that the complete list of data consists of pairs of items, the first item in each pair being used as an index to the second. The second item can itself be a list of any complexity. Chapter 1 showed how the data tree could be stored as such pairs, with an atom at the head, and a list of two elements in the tail. These were called triples in that chapter. The association list itself is sometimes called an Alist in LISP.

Recall that the complete association list of Figure 1.1 in Chapter 1 may be written as:

```
( (heavenly-body (star-like planet-like))
  (star-like (single-point galaxy-shaped))
  (planet-like (planet moon))
  (planet (Earth not-Earth))
  (Earth)
  ( . . . . . . .
```

This is only the start of the knowledge base for this system, and the user must be able to add to this whenever he wishes. In addition, he must be able to use it to identify a given heavenly-body from the simple YES/NO question and answer procedure. This requires two programs, and we will look at both shortly.

To retrieve any piece of data from the knowledge base above we will need a special function called ASSOC. This is defined next.

ASSOC

ASSOC is a function which picks out sublists from a database list of the form of the one above for Figure 1.1. It retrieves sublist elements from the database by looking for the head of the required sublist. It is used as follows:

```
(ASSOC   index-element   data-base-list)
```

This has a value equal to the sublist with the given index-element at its head. To use ASSOC, the first thing to do is to bind the complete database-list to an identifier. We will use KBASE, which is short for Knowledge Base. You should use SETQ to set KBASE to the heavenly-body list above. Do not forget to use a QUOTE.

To retrieve the data associated with planet-like in KBASE, type in:

```
(ASSOC 'planet-like KBASE)
```

This will cause KBASE to be searched for a member sublist with planet-like at its head. The whole member will be retrieved, so the value will be:

```
(planet-like (planet moon))
```

We can then use CAR and CDR a few times to find planet and moon from this. If triples containing plant and moon were stored in the knowledge base, ASSOC could then be used on them to find the next pieces of data in the tree along the next two branches, if required. If CDR of this list had been NIL, it would have meant that a branch ending had been found. For instance, the following gives NIL:

```
(CDR (ASSOC 'Earth KBASE))
```

It will be convenient to define two more simple functions for this procedure. The branches from a node are very important to the use of KBASE, and we will define LBRANCH and RBRANCH to equal the (atomic) ends of the left and right branches emanating from a given node respectively. For instance, the LBRANCH from heavenly-body is star-like, and the RBRANCH from planet is not-Earth. You can see these directly from the tree diagram, or from KBASE above.

Before continuing, try to define LBRANCH and RBRANCH for yourself.

Branch endings - **LBRANCH and RBRANCH**

To define these two new functions, let us examine a typical use of ASSOC. Type in the following:

```
(ASSOC 'planet KBASE)
```

This returns the value:

```
(planet (Earth not-Earth))
```

The CDR of this is:

```
((Earth not-Earth))
```

Note the double brackets. CDR is always a list, unless dealing with dotted pairs, and here the CDR has a single element which happens to be a list. To produce Earth from this, it is tempting to try to use CAR on this, or to produce not-Earth one might try CDR. Neither of these will work on this value. CAR looks at the first element, which is the list:

```
(Earth not-Earth)
```

and CDR cannot find a tail – it gives NIL.

In order to produce Earth, you must use CAR twice after CDR on KBASE. Thus, the LBRANCH is equal to:

```
(CAADR (ASSOC 'planet KBASE))
```

To see how to produce the RBRANCH, consider:

```
(CDADR (ASSOC 'planet KBASE))
```

You should be clear that this gives (not-Earth) before continuing. Thus we need to take the CAR of this list to finally produce an atom which is the RBRANCH. Thus RBRANCH equals:

```
(CAR (CDADR (ASSOC 'planet KBASE)))
```

The general definitions of these two branch functions should include the case where the index is not found, and where the branches are NIL as for Earth. The first of these possibilities depends upon the action of your particular LISP. If the index is not found, as would be the case if you were to type in:

```
(ASSOC 'Hello KBASE)
```

some LISPs will return NIL for ASSOC, and some will return the last sublist stored. If the latter is the case, you will have to add an end of list member – something like (END) – and use this to signal that the index being searched has not been found. You can experiment with your LISP and see what does happen here.

We will simply assume that the database and program is constructed to ensure that this situation never arises. In other words, the database must be fully closed before the program acts on it. All branches must go somewhere, which is the same as saying that the LBRANCH and RBRANCH values must appear somewhere else in KBASE – that is, unless one of them is NIL. The case where an index is followed by the empty list is very important here, and must be allowed for.

To allow for cases such as (Earth), the sublist produced by ASSOC must be tested directly to see if it is a singleton list. If it is, LBRANCH and RBRANCH must return NIL. The following definitions achieve this:

```
(DEFUN LBRANCH (index KBASE)
      (SETQ X (ASSOC index KBASE))
      (COND ( (NULL (CDR X)) NIL )
            (T (CAADR X)))))

(DEFUN RBRANCH (index KBASE)
      (SETQ X (ASSOC index KBASE))
      (COND ( (NULL (CDR X)) NIL )
            (T (CAR (CDADR (ASSOC index KBASE)))))))
```

A further refinement to these definitions concerns the use of the global variable X. It may be that X is used outside these functions, and will be interfered with by LBRANCH and RBRANCH. X should not be declared as an argument to force it to be local, or some value will have to be input for it each time the functions are used. This will work perfectly well, but is a waste of time.

There are three solutions. The first is to reserve generally a number of special identifiers which you always use as dummy variables, and never rely on to be left untouched by your functions. This is a good general rule anyway, and variables such as X1, X2, X3, etc. fulfill this purpose admirably. Simply replace X by one of these in the above definitions.

The second solution is to try to use one of the local variables within the function if possible. This can be done here by replacing X by KBASE or index. Either of these will do, as they are only used once to transfer the input values of the index and the database being used to ASSOC, and they are then free for use.

The third solution is LISP dialect dependent. Most LISPs have a method of declaring local variables within a function which are not required as arguments. We will look at this again in Chapter 6. For the moment, we will use one of the above two solutions.

The two branch functions can now be used to write one of the required programs.

Database maintenance

We need a routine which allows the user to fill the database from scratch, or add new data in. It does not matter where the new data pairs are stored within the database, and a convenient place to put it is at the head of the list using CONS. Thus, a new data list is input using READ, and stored to KBASE using CONS. This is done in a loop which is exited when you type in a particular input such as END, for instance.

Example 4.1
Construct this last function which we shall call DBADD. Assume that it takes a database as its argument, and allows a new triple to be input from the keyboard to the head of the list. The process repeats until END is typed in.

Example 4.2
Another important facility for maintenance of the database is to be able to delete a given entry. This is done using the DELETE function which some LISPs might have already. The function is used as follows:

(DELETE ELEMENT L)

The function returns the list L, omitting the first occurrence of the value ELEMENT if it is included in L.

The DELETE function will not go inside any sublists of the given list, but in general, it can be used to delete members of the given list which are themselves lists. This is exactly what we need here for members of KBASE. However, until we can actually compare two lists, using an equivalent of EQ for general lists, this definition of DELETE will have to wait. It will be defined in the next chapter.

For now, assume that the value of ELEMENT above is an atom, and to make the task easier, assume that the list L is not empty. Construct this function, and call it DEL instead of DELETE.

As a clue, the problem is solved by taking the elements of L one at a time, by repetitively stripping off the head. Each element is compared to ELEMENT, and CONSRed to a list variable if not equal to ELEMENT. If it is equal to ELEMENT, the first occurrence of ELEMENT has been found, and the rest of L must be APPENDed onto the list variable built up so far.

You should begin by drawing a flowchart, and if you cannot think how to start, have a look at the flowchart given in the answer at the back of this chapter.

Now try DEL out on some examples of your own. Remember that it is to remove just the first occurrence of the given element. If the element is not present in the list, DEL simply returns the list untouched.

The search program

The program to use the database starts at the triple stored in **KBASE** which is defined as the first element. This is heavenly-body. It then follows the left or right branches according to the outcome of YES/NO questions. You can make the whole program more sophisticated yourself, once you have the basic routine to play with.

Figure 4.1 shows the bare bones of a program to search through the database. It depends upon the entire database being closed. In other words, all branches must lead somewhere. The short database given above for Figure 1.1, which is called **KBASE**, is not closed. For instance, single-point does not lead anywhere. To close that branch, you would have to add either an ending list such as (single-point) or a new triple with single-point in the head.

We will assume that the database is closed before we search it. Let us now examine Figure 4.1.

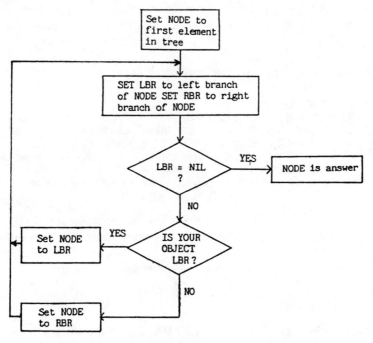

Fig. 4.1 Flowchart for PLAY-GAME

The first action is to set the variable NODE to the first element in the tree. Then using LBRANCH and RBRANCH, set LBR and RBR to the elements at the ends of the two branches coming from NODE. If LBR is NIL, then NODE must be a branch ending, and the game is over, with NODE storing the answer. If LBR is not NIL, then it is used to ask a question. You may have noticed that all the tree elements are written so that you can ask the questions of the form:

is your object LBR ?

and you can answer YES or NO to this question. For instance, here LBR is actually star-like. The game's first question, then, is:

is your object star-like?

If the answer is YES, NODE must be set to star-like, i.e. to LBR. If not, it must be set to RBR. Either way, the loop starts again by finding the LBR and RBR of this new NODE. The loop continues until it finds an ending branch.

You should now close KBASE by adding some new triples to ensure that every atom in the tail of every triple indexes another triple, even if that triple only contains the index.

Try to code the game into a LISP function called PLAY-GAME before continuing. Assume that PLAY-GAME takes no arguments. At the start, do not concern yourself with the look of the screen. The first program you write will probably not even ask any questions. It will simply look blank, and expect you to know what to input next. The program below has the minimum of screen output, with just enough for you to understand the program's use.

The following is the program implied by Figure 4.1:

```
(DEFUN PLAY-GAME ()
   (SETQ NODE 'heavenly-body)
   (LOOP (SETQ LBR (LBRANCH NODE KBASE))
         (SETQ RBR (RBRANCH NODE KBASE))
         (UNTIL (NULL LBR) (PRINT 'answer-is- NODE))
         (PRINT 'is-your-object- LBR)
         (COND ((EQ (READ) 'YES) (SETQ NODE LBR))
               (T (SETQ NODE RBR))))))
```

Note that there are spaces after the lower-case message atoms above to separate them from the variables which follow and which are evaluated before printing. This assumes that your LISP allows PRINT to have more than one argument – otherwise use two PRINTs or look up your manual.

To use the program, simply type in:

(PLAY-GAME)

There are no arguments in the DEFUN, and hence no arguments are required here.

The program is best understood by regarding it as having a number of levels, and this is how the program is actually set out above. Once you can see the levels for yourself, you will be able to add to it, and make it more sophisticated. The outer level contains two lists. The first list is headed by a SETQ, and the second by a LOOP. Then within the LOOP list, there are five further lists. These are two SETQs, an UNTIL, a PRINT and a COND. Some of these have further levels within them. For instance, The UNTIL has two expressions to be evaluated. The COND contains two lists, both headed by predicates, of course, and each of these lists has further expressions within it.

If you match the flowchart up with the program above, its working should be clear.

Extensions

To extend the program, you could add a PRINT after the SETQ RBR expression in the LOOP list. Try adding bits to the program until it is more pleasant to use.

As you use DBADD and PLAY-GAME, you will come up against a number of problems. You should try to analyse how these problems arise, and how to find a way around them by improving the programs.

This shows a useful example of the type of use to which the ASSOC function can be put. It allows you to code a tree of data in a simple and extensible form for use by list processing routines.

As an example for you to have a go at, it is useful to be able to add more than two branches to any given node. How would you change the programs to allow for this?

Association lists are comparatively simple methods of storing large quantities of data in a highly structured and retrievable form. However, to store data in an indexed manner, without the complexity of a complete tree, there is another, and simpler, method of storing data in LISP. This is called the property list, and is described in the next section.

Property lists – PUT and GET

It is important to be able to retrieve data easily and quickly from a database using an index of some kind. This use of the database as a fast automatic filing cabinet is probably its most common application. It would be useful, for instance, to be able to retrieve all the appointments written on a given diary page, indexed by date. Or, the complete personal details of a given person could be retrieved from a large file of data indexed by name. It would also be useful if you could simply type in a person's name, plus the word WEIGHT, say, and the person's weight would appear, without your having

properties→ identifiers↓	ADDRESS	PHONE-NO	HEIGHT	WEIGHT	FOOD-HATES
JOHN-SMITH	4 RED RD LONDON NW6	3215672	70	165	LIVER BACON CABBAGE

Fig. 4.2 JOHN-SMITH's property list

to wade through his personal file to find the data. It is with this type of requirement in mind that the concept of a property list is defined in LISP.

In a property list, data is stored by LISP in a manner which is not important to the user. All he cares about is that data may be stored and retrieved using the PUT and GET functions. The actual data is not available as a linked list, as it was for ASSOC; it is simply stored in drawers in a filing cabinet for later use.

Each identifier in LISP may have a list of any number of properties associated with it in a property list. These properties do not affect the identifier, but are simply attached to it no matter what may happen.

As an example, consider the atom JOHN-SMITH. There are many properties which people have, including address, phone number, height, weight, food hates, and so on. Figure 4.2 shows a property list for JOHN-SMITH, in a matrix very like a standard entry in a card index. For a few people, this is small and instantly manageable, but imagine having to deal with hundreds of people, and dozens of properties. LISP can store these with great ease, and allow you to retrieve any property of any person instantly.

To put in the data of Figure 4.2, we use the PUT function, which takes three arguments. The general form of the function is:

```
(PUT   identifier   property   value)
```

Here, the identifier may be JOHN-SMITH, the property FOOD-HATES, and the value:

```
(LIVER BACON CABBAGE)
```

Thus, this piece of data is input using:

```
(PUT  'JOHN-SMITH  'FOOD-HATES  '(LIVER BACON CABBAGE)
```

To retrieve this particular property of JOHN-SMITH, we use the function GET, which takes two arguments, and has the general form:

```
(GET   identifier   property)
```

This returns the value of the property. Thus, the above list of food hates would be the value of:

```
(GET  'JOHN-SMITH  'FOOD-HATES)
```

As you can see, it is remarkably easy to store and retrieve the data held in this manner. There are as many applications for this type of structure as there are ways of using a card index, or any other form of filing system.

Before looking at an example, it is important to be able to remove properties from the property list of an identifier, as well as add them. For this, your LISP should have a function called REMPROP which does just that. It takes two arguments, exactly as for GET. Thus:

```
(REMPROP 'JOHN-SMITH 'WEIGHT)
```

will remove the data of WEIGHT from JOHN-SMITH's property list. In fact, in some LISPs the whole property is removed, and in others the data under that property heading is set to NIL. This is a minor difference, and you can check it for yourself. It is irrelevant, as whether you GET a property which does not exist, or one which is set to NIL, the answer is the same – NIL.

It is also useful to be able to list all the properties of an identifier. This is usually done with the function PLIST, which takes just the identifier as its argument. If you type in the data of Figure 4.2, and then try

```
(PLIST 'JOHN-SMITH)
```

you will be able to see how your LISP stores the data on the property list. Try saving a few more properties, and removing some using REMPROP before continuing. This will be helpful in making the use of property lists clear for the next example.

An automated diary

We use files of data in many parts of our everyday life, even if not actually for our work. One of the most common is the diary. The example below shows how to automate your diary using LISP.

The main problem is to decide on the exact method of storage. There are two main possibilities, and these are shown in Figure 4.3. The first is to

properties→ identifiers↓	D01-01-86	D02-01-86	D03-01-86	D04-01-86	etc.
DIARY	VALUE	VALUE	VALUE	VALUE	etc.

properties→ identifiers↓	APPT 1	APPT 2	APPT 3	APPT 4	etc.
D01-01-86 D02-01-86 D03-01-86 etc.	VALUE VALUE	VALUE			

Fig. 4.3 The diary properties list

choose a single identifier such as DIARY, and use the actual dates as the property names. The values of the properties would be the data stored on each page of the diary. The second method would be to use the dates as the identifiers, and APPT1, APPT2, etc. as the properties. The data stored on each page would be more easily changed in this latter case, without having to change the whole page. We will use the first method here, and the exercise for you to try is to rewrite the program to use the second method.

Each property on the property list of DIARY will be called something like:

03-01-86 or D03-01-86

The point is that the actual date itself must be encoded in the property name, and the exact details of this will depend upon your LISP. If you are allowed to use identifiers which start with a number, then the first identifier will work. If you are not, then you will have to put a letter at the start, and follow it with the date as shown. It is important that you stick religiously to a consistent method of labelling the diary pages. We shall therefore use the second identifier shown, for safety, and follow the D with two digits for the day, a hyphen, two digits for the month, another hyphen and two digits for the year.

To put a page of data into the property list for the 13th of January 1986, you could simply type in:

(PUT 'DIARY 'D13-01-86 '(10-30 AM meet Bob at station 2-15 PM – Meeting at head office – Dont forget Peters birthday present))

You should be a little careful of the exact details of the data to be put into the property list. Do not forget that it is just an ordinary list. Do not use punctuation marks, or other special symbols in the list, or your particular LISP may throw up an error. If you have typed this in, try using GET to ensure that the data has been accepted correctly.

To produce a program for the diary, we will define a function called PAGE which will take a date as its argument. You will be able to rewrite the associated diary page, including wiping it out by using NIL, or simply recall the page, for reading.

PAGE has to start off by asking whether you wish to read or write to the page. It then uses GET or PUT to perform the task. A simple program for this would be:

```
(DEFUN PAGE (DATE)
    (LOOP (PRINT) (PRINT 'READ-OR-WRITE)
          (SETQ X1 (READ))
          (UNTIL (EQ X1 'READ)
                 (PRINT) (PRINT 'YOUR-ENTRY-ON- DATE 'IS)
                 (PRINT) (PRINT (GET 'DIARY DATE)))
          (UNTIL (EQ X1 'WRITE)
                 (PRINT) (PRINT 'INPUT-YOUR-ENTRY)
                 (PUT 'DIARY DATE (READ)))))
```

If you type this in, you will be able to set up a straightforward diary of dates and general information. As you can see, the whole program is confined to a loop. This is purely to allow for wrong inputs from the keyboard in response to the printed message READ-OR-WRITE. If you respond with READ, the GET is used to retrieve the page for that day. If you type in WRITE, PUT is used to store your entry, completely overwriting the data on the page. If some other word is typed in by mistake, the loop passes round again, and once again prompts for READ or WRITE. Again, PRINT here is assumed to allow multiple arguments.

You should be able to refine this program considerably, and if you use the other method of storing the data, you will be able to rewrite parts of a given day, instead of destroying the complete page for any given date.

We will now look at a few more special LISP functions, to complete your knowledge of the 'nuts and bolts' of the language.

EXPLODE and IMPLODE

On occasion, it is useful to be able to analyse an atom as a list of its characters. For instance, in the area of natural language interpretation, a given word may appear in a number of forms which only differ by the last few letters. Therefore, some words can be matched up by comparing all but their last two or three letters. A good example of this is in the normal plural ending of nouns. The words GATE and GATES are to be generally regarded as referring to the same type of object. A language interpreter would have to recognise and understand this fact, as well as appreciating the difference.

To do this, the words have to taken apart, matched letter by letter, and it has to be noted that they differ by just the plural ending. The first step is to form a list of their constituent letters. EXPLODE does exactly that. EXPLODE takes a single non-numeric atom (identifier) as argument, and produces a list of its characters. For instance:

```
(EXPLODE 'hello)  gives  (h e l l o)
```

Also, if X is set to HELLO, say, then

```
(EXPLODE  X)    gives   (H E L L O)
```

The opposite function to this is called IMPLODE, and it effectively removes the spaces between members of a list. The members do not have to be separate characters, but they must not be lists. IMPLODE can be used as follows:

```
(IMPLODE '(H E L L O))  has value: HELLO

(IMPLODE '(H ELL O))    has value:  HELLO

(IMPLODE '(well hello there)) has value:  wellhellothere
```

Example 4.3
As an example of the use of this facility, define a function which we will call
MATCHPLU. It will take two arguments, which will be identifiers, and give
the value T for words which match up apart from an S for a plural ending,
and NIL otherwise. Assume that the words are entirely in upper-case. As a
clue, you can do it using the function REVERSE from the last chapter, or
using CONSR, but you do not need both.

Example 4.4
Using computers interactively quickly makes it clear that most computer
programs are remarkably stupid. If you mistype a word, the computer will
give an error, or completely misunderstand your input. Humans do not,
generally, suffer from this very 'black and white' view of language, and
intelligent programs should not either – unless accuracy is important in the
given context.

To help in understanding words which are nearly the same, we need a new
function which will compare two words, and return one of three possible
answers. T is returned if they are exactly the same, NIL if they differ by more
than one character in any given position in the word, and NEAR if they
differ by just one character. This exercise is to define a function called
NEARMATCH which does this when given two atoms as arguments which
are the words to be compared.

To make the exercise easier, assume that the words have the same number
of letters.

The clue is that the words are compared by exploding them, stripping off
their heads one by one, and comparing these.

Try to define the function so that it can be extended easily to include three
or four characters different before returning NIL. Assume that letter
position is important – i.e. that words such as GRATES and GYRATE
differ by five characters, even though they have almost the same letters in
them, and that they are even largely in the same order. The point is that only
the G at the beginning of these words is actually the same and in the same
position.

Finally, you should certainly draw a flowchart before starting, and if you
need a further clue as to how to write the program, there is a flowchart in the
solution to this problem at the end of this chapter.

Two more list functions RPLACA and RPLACD

RPLACA and RPLACD are used to replace the CAR and CDR
respectively of a list. They act by actually changing the memory pointers of
the data in the list. This may seem a rather academic point, but you will see
that it has a rather dangerous effect, which makes it important that you use
these functions with great care.

RPLACA and RPLACD have the general form:

```
(RPLACA list new-CAR)    and    (RPLACD list new-CDR)
```

Try the following examples to see them working:
Start off with:

```
(SETQ L '(Peter jumped the gate))
```

Then try:

```
(RPLACA L 'John)
```

Some LISPs return the new list, and some return just the replaced part. It is irrelevant because the action of RPLACA here is actually to affect L itself. Thus, whatever the last line returned, if you now examine L, you will find that it has been replaced by:

```
(John jumped the gate)
```

The point is that this is one of the few functions we have encountered that actually changes one of its arguments. SETQ is another, of course.

Now using this new value for L, type in:

```
(RPLACD L '(likes jam))
```

and then type in L to see the result. As you can see, L has been changed to:

```
(John likes jam)
```

These functions are quite useful for altering lists without having to use an extra SETQ function. For instance, to change the head of the list:

```
(A B C)      ---
```

stored in the variable L, we would normally use something like:

```
(CONS 'X (CDR L))
```

This has the correct value:

```
(X B C)
```

which will be printed on the screen, quite correctly. However, if you now examine L, it is, of course, unchanged. If you want it changed, you have to use:

```
(SETQ L (CONS 'X (CDR L)))
```

and now L itself will have its head changed.

The last line can be written considerably more neatly by:

```
(RPLACA L 'X)
```

which simply replaces the head of L with X directly.

Just remember that these functions are like SETQ, and you will have no trouble with them – in fact, you will find them very useful.

Summary

Association list. This is a list of sublists. Each sublist has a head which is called its index. This is used to retrieve that sublist using ASSOC, when the whole sublist is retrieved, with all the data in its tail. By this means, a whole tree of data can be stored as a very economical and easily handled linked list. *ASSOC* takes two arguments. The first is the index atom, and the second the association list being referred to. ASSOC has value equal to the whole sublist retrieved.

Property list. A list of data referenced to a given atom, by storing data under subheadings for that atom. The analogy is a card index, with the atom as its overall name, and subheadings, each of which has a card of data stored against it.

PUT takes an atom, a subheading (or property) followed by the value to be stored as arguments.

GET takes just the atomic name followed by the property to be read as arguments, and has the value of that property as its value.

RPLACA removes the head of a list, and replaces it with another. It takes the list followed by the new head as arguments. Actually it changes its first argument, as does SETQ.

RPLACD is exactly as for RPLACA, but replaces tail.

Solutions to problems

Example 4.1 – DBADD

A simple function for adding new data to the database would be:

```
(DEFUN DBADD (KBASE)
       (LOOP (PRINT 'INPUT-NEXT-ITEM)
             (SETQ X (READ))
             (UNTIL (EQ X 'END) KBASE)
             (SETQ KBASE (CONS X KBASE)))))
```

This certainly adds the required data, but does not make the changes permanent. This is due to the fact that KBASE is a local variable here, and the actual database itself is thus left untouched. DBADD actually returns the value of the altered database as its value. To make the changes permanent, you will have to use:

```
(SETQ KBASE (DBADD KBASE))
```

This is a typical problem with using functions. A routine will often look as if it is achieving an end, but is actually purely local to the inside of the routine itself. This is why the UNTIL expression above has a KBASE in it, to return the completed database to the function. Also, the last line of the function definition uses a SETQ to cause the changes to be made to the local database.

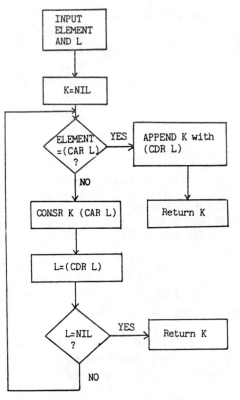

Fig. 4.4 Flowchart for DEL

This function is very simple, and its printed messages rather rudimentary. You should examine your own LISP and see how the printed messages could be improved. Then rewrite the program to give some better screen handling. Also, if you misstype your data in certain ways while using this program, you may produce an error and all the data typed in up to that point will be lost. How can you prevent this from happening? The clue is that the problem is due to KBASE being local to DBADD.

Example 4.2 – DEL

The flowchart of Figure 4.4 sets out the process of defining DEL. The value to be returned is either the list L, or the list L with the first occurrence of ELEMENT missing, if ELEMENT is in L. The final version of L will be built up in the variable K, and the first expression in the program is to set K to NIL to ensure that it is not undefined when it is needed.

The CAR of L is then checked to see if it equals ELEMENT. If not, this CAR is added to the end of K, which in this first loop pass simply produces a singleton list in K. The head is then stripped off L by setting it to its own CDR. If L is NIL at this point, then K contains the answer, and the program ends, returning K.

If L is not NIL, ELEMENT is again compared with the CAR. If not, the CAR is added onto the end of K, and this produces a new list containing the first two elements of L, in the correct order. L is again checked for NIL, and if not the process repeats until either L is NIL, or ELEMENT is found.

If ELEMENT is found to be equal to the CAR of L, K is appended to CDR of L, in order to leave out this CAR. This produces the final value of DEL to be returned.

The program itself is given below:

```
(DEFUN DEL (ELEMENT L)
   (SETQ K NIL)
   (LOOP (UNTIL (EQ ELEMENT (CAR L))
                (APPEND K (CDR L)) )
         (SETQ K (CONSR K (CAR L)))
         (SETQ L (CDR L))
         (UNTIL (NULL L) K)))
```

This function starts by setting K to NIL, and then enters a loop. The loop may be exited at the start if ELEMENT is at the head of L, and the expression following this predicate is the APPEND shown in the flowchart. As this is the last expression evaluated, it is returned as the value of DEL, as required.

The rest of the loop is exactly as on the flowchart, and the final UNTIL will exit if L is reduced to NIL. Again, the last expression evaluated is K itself, and this is passed to DEL, and returned.

Example 4.3 - MATCHPLU

MATCHPLU is defined in one of two ways. First, the two words are exploded, and then reversed. They are checked to see whether either has an S as its CAR. If not, this function does not apply, and NIL is returned. If one has an S as its CAR, the S is stripped off, and the words imploded, to allow them to be compared using EQ, which cannot be used for lists in this context.

Note that this gives NIL for two words which are exactly the same. It is easy to add a check for this possibility in the definition of MATCHPLU, but it will be assumed that the program using MATCHPLU has checked for this possibility before MATCHPLU is called.

The other way that MATCHPLU could be defined would be to add an S onto the end of one of the words, and then use EQ to see if that had made them the same. The same could then be tried for the other word. If one of these succeeds, then the two words only differ by an S at the end. To add the S onto the end of a word, it must first be exploded, then CONSR is used, then imploded for EQ.

The solution program using REVERSE is as follows:

```
(DEFUN MATCHPLU (WORD1 WORD2)
   (SETQ WORD1 (REVERSE (EXPLODE WORD1)))
   (SETQ WORD2 (REVERSE (EXPLODE WORD2)))
```

```
(COND ((AND (EQ (CAR WORD1) 'S)
            (EQ (IMPLODE (CDR WORD1))
                (IMPLODE WORD2)))    T )
      ((AND (EQ (CAR WORD2) 'S)
            (EQ (IMPLODE (CDR WORD2))
                (IMPLODE WORD1)))    T )
      (T NIL)))
```

Again, to understand this, you must look at it as a set of levels. The first level has three lists in it – two SETQs and a COND. The SETQs simply explode and then reverse the given words, so that CAR can be used to expose the S's which may be at the ends of the words. No external variables are used here, and so no interference will be caused with any other routines.

The COND has three lists within it. The first list checks for the condition that CAR of WORD1 is S and CDR of WORD1 equals WORD2. If both of these facts are true, the COND returns T, and the function ends with this value. The second list in the COND checks the words the other way round. The final list in COND is only entered if the words do not differ by just an ending S, and thus it returns the value NIL.

The other method of defining MATCHPLU is as follows:

```
(DEFUN MATCHPLU (WORD1 WORD2)
    (SETQ WORD1 (EXPLODE WORD1))
    (SETQ WORD2 (EXPLODE WORD2))
    (COND ((EQ (IMPLODE WORD1)
               (IMPLODE (CONSR WORD2 'S))) T)
          ((EQ (IMPLODE WORD2)
               (IMPLODE (CONSR WORD1 'S))) T)
          (T NIL)))
```

This is a slightly simpler program than the last one. Again the words are first exploded, and then operated upon. The COND again has three expressions. The first returns T to the function if adding an S to WORD2 makes it equal to WORD1. The second COND expression does the same the other way round. The final expression of COND only comes into play if neither of the preceding has returned T to the function. It always returns NIL.

There are other ways to write this last program. In particular, you should spend a little time trying to make it more efficient, and written in a smaller space.

Example 4.4 – NEARMATCH

The trick with NEARMATCH is to explode the given words, strip off the heads one by one and compare them. The differences are counted, and when two is reached, the function finishes and returns NIL. Otherwise one of the other values is returned. There are many approaches to the programming of any function other than the very simplest types. The solution is by no means unique, and one of the best exercises you can set yourself is to try to think of other ways to solve the problem.

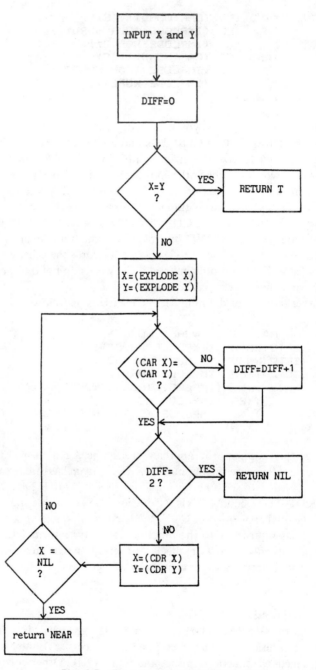

Fig. 4.5 Flowchart for NEARMATCH

Figure 4.5 gives a flowchart for a solution to the process. X and Y are the local variables containing the input words. The differences are counted in a variable called DIFF, which is set to zero to start with. Before going any further, X and Y are compared, and if they are equal, the function ends, and T is returned as required.

If X and Y are not equal, they are exploded. Their CARs are then compared, and DIFF is incremented if they differ.

If DIFF equals 2, then the function ends, and returns NIL. This not the case in the first pass of the loop, however, and X and Y are then set to their CDRs. As X and Y are of the same length, you can check either X or Y to see whether stripping off the heads has given an empty list. If so, the process is finished. If the loop ends here, DIFF cannot be 2, or it would have ended before, and DIFF cannot be 0 or it would have ended at the start where X and Y were compared. Thus, DIFF must be 1, and the value NEAR is returned.

If the loop does not end here, the loop repeats, and continues until either DIFF equals 2, or X is empty.

To extend this to allow for more than 2 differences, simply change the second decision box in Figure 4.5 to asking if DIFF equals a larger number. The loop will still return NEAR for any other non-zero number as before.

The program which goes with the flowchart is as follows:

```
(DEFUN NEARMATCH (X Y)
   (SETQ DIFF 0)
   (COND ((EQ X Y) T)
         (T  (SETQ X (EXPLODE X))
             (SETQ Y (EXPLODE Y))
             (LOOP (COND ((NOT (EQ (CAR X) (CAR Y)))
                                (SETQ DIFF (PLUS DIFF 1))))
                   (UNTIL (EQ DIFF 2) NIL)
                   (SETQ X (CDR X))
                   (SETQ Y (CDR Y))
                   (UNTIL (NULL X) 'NEAR)))))
```

There is only one slightly subtle point about this program which may have thrown you. It concerns the fact that most of the program is contained within the COND. The rest is just hard work, and a repeat of everything before.

The DEFUN has only two lists in the body of the function. The first sets DIFF to zero; the second is a COND function which contains the rest of the program.

To produce the first decision box in Figure 4.5, the COND must present two alternatives. Either X and Y are equal, in which case the COND must finish and return T; or X and Y or not equal, and the rest of the program is run. If the COND finishes here, the next function after the COND list is entered and executed. However, as you can see, there is nothing after the COND list, so the whole program ends, returning the value of COND which is T here. If the rest of the program were not actually contained within the COND, then it would be run when the COND finishes, instead.

If X and Y are different, the T alternative of the COND is entered, and X and Y are exploded.

The next step is to enter the LOOP part of the program which is contained within the LOOP list, as shown.

By now, the indentations should be of considerable help to you, though it may not be efficient to type your programs in this way with your particular LISP.

The LOOP is comparatively straightforward, and similar to all the other loops we have seen. It has two UNTIL exits, one of which returns NIL to the function, while the other returns NEAR.

Pick your way through this program, and make sure you understand it. You should then think of ways of expanding it a little as suggested.

Chapter Five
Recursion

Introduction

As you will know by now, functions are at the basis of LISP programming. LISP generally encourages you to split large processes into separate functions, each of which becomes an internal part of LISP for later use in any other functions.

The complexity and subtlety of the use of functions which is offered by your LISP package will very much determine its particular usefulness. However, there is one functional facility which all LISPs include, and that is *recursion*. It is a special type of iteration, and this is how it will be introduced here.

Recursion is one of the most maligned and misunderstood facilities in programming. Some writers lead you to believe that a programming language without it is useless, others tell you that it is the most difficult procedure ever invented, and others tell you that you cannot do any AI without it.

These views are rather extreme. The truth is that recursion is a very useful addition to any language, and it is good at simplifying list processing functions – hence its use in AI. It is also true that it is not as easy to pick up as many of the procedures you have met so far in programming. Its difficulty arises mainly from one mental block which we all suffer when meeting this type of procedure for the first time. The aim here is to show you where this point is, and hopefully help you to conquer it. You should read the chapter carefully, and try out all the examples.

Iteration in general

Iteration simply means performing a set of activities over and over again, perhaps with some values changed. The use of LOOP is an example of iteration, but not the only one. Recursion is another, in a certain sense.

As you will probably already know BASIC, and now you know nearly all of LISP, iteration should be very clear to you. As an example, let us look at the definition of APPEND from Chapter 3. To look at the iteration in that definition, let us forget the DEFUN, and look at the inner process. It is reproduced here to save you turning back and forth to that chapter. Remember that L and K are lists to be combined to form a larger list.

```
(LOOP (UNTIL (NULL K) L)
      (SETQ L (CONSR L (CAR K)))
      (SETQ K (CDR K)))
```

The essence of the iteration here is that the head of K is stripped off, and added to the right-hand end of L. This process is then repeated until K is empty. The repeated process is the stripping from K, and gluing to L. We can actually watch this iteration being performed by putting PRINT expressions into the loop if we wish. Each expression is evaluated as many times as there are elements in K. The loop is clear and open for all to see.

You will have to bear this example in mind below, as we shall define APPEND using recursion soon so that you can compare the two.

In fact, you will see that recursion uses a mathematical procedure to trick the computer into looping. Read on!

Induction

To understand a different form of iteration from the one above, it is useful to look at a simple but powerful mathematical procedure called *induction*.

Consider the following statement: 'A list containing any number of atoms can be built up from its atoms by the repetitive use of CONS'

This statement is important as it gives a clue as to how to build up lists from their elements. It may either seem obvious to you, or you may feel that it is actually not true, i.e. that there are some lists, composed of atoms, which cannot be made up simply by using CONS on atoms.

How would you set about proving the statement? Would you simply take any old list, and show how to construct it from atoms using CONS? Most of us probably would. However, this does not constitute a proof – just an example.

Consider making the following statement on a rainy winter's day: 'It rains everyday, without fail, in winter'. If example were a proof, that proof would be just outside the window, even though we know the statement to be false.

To prove the statement about lists and CONS, above, we could try to construct every single list of atoms in this way, to prove they can all be done. Unfortunately, though, there is not enough time left to our present universe to take this process to its full conclusion!

The method of proof which is chosen here is to start with the smallest list possible, and consider building upwards to a general list. Once we have taken this decision, we should look at singleton lists first, and try a proof just for them.

A proof for singletons is easy; just construct a general singleton. Thus the proof starts with the statement:

(i) Any singleton set, (A), satisfies the statement.

The proof is in the LISP expression:

```
(CONS 'A NIL)
```

This has value (A), and thus proves the statement for all singleton lists in existence, because A is a completely general atom. You could go on and use the same logic to prove it for doubletons, and so on, but this is not necessary, as we shall see.

The next step in induction is to consider a general list, of any length, and assume that by some miracle the statement to be proven is already true for that list. In other words, the list has actually been built up using CONS as required. The trick is to show that the next higher list, with one more element, can be built up from this using CONS. In other words, try to prove:

(ii) A list L, with a given number of elements, and which does satisfy the statement, can be built into a higher list for which the statement is true.

This is proven by

```
(CONS 'A L)
```

for any general atom A which is required.

As (ii) is true, we can now show that any list can be built up by starting with a singleton. This goes as follows:

Because the statement is true for singletons, (ii) above tells you that it is also true for the next higher lists – doubletons. If it is true for doubletons, (ii) again shows it must be true for triples, and then for quartets and so on until the given list is reached. You do not actually have to perform the process; it is assured if (ii) above is true.

As you can see, this is a sort of iteration, where you do not actually have to perform the iterative process. You start it off, go to a general part of it, and do just that single iteration, and the whole iteration is effectively done.

Note also that the actual method of using (ii) to produce, say, the list (A B C D E F), from a list with one less element, only works if you take L as the CDR of this list, as CONS only adds the extra element to the head of the list. However, any list can certainly be built up from scratch by this induction, as long as you choose the correct atoms, and thus the whole statement is proven.

The central point to remember is that in (ii) we assumed that the CONS statement was already true, before we had proven it. However, by putting this aside for a short time we were able to produce a complete proof. This is recursion – the use of the result itself, to prove the result, and it is here that most people's mental blocks occur. Do not let this happen to you!

Before moving on to recursion, we will just state the processes of induction in a more general form:

(i) Do the process for the simplest case
(ii) Assume a general case, and build up the next one.

Recursion

Recursion is a method of using a result to prove or define itself. A *recursive definition* is one where a thing is defined in terms of itself, but this process must be started somewhere, as for induction.

For instance, a recursive definition of a list would be:

A list is a collection of atoms or lists separated by spaces, and contained in round brackets.

The important question is – can we construct all known lists from this definition? The answer is yes. You start with the bit which says, effectively, a collection of atoms is a list, and thus we have constructed one whole class of lists – the ones with no sublists. This is, effectively, the start of an induction. The next step is to note that the definition includes lists within the list, thus a collection of atoms and lists of atoms is a list. Then note that, by the definition, this new type of list can also be a member of a list, and so on as far as you like. In this manner you can construct any type of list you can write down from this definition.

This is not mathematically rigorous, but it shows the point, which is that recursion is using something to define itself.

Recursive definitions of functions

In LISP, recursion is used to define functions. In the previous chapters, we used loops and other mechanisms within the body of DEFUN. We shall see that the same functions, and many others, can be defined more neatly using recursion.

As an example, we will return to the definition of APPEND, and rewrite it using the iterative process of recursion.

In fact, recursion and induction are the same thing, and if you remember the procedure of induction, you will have no trouble in defining functions recursively.

To define (APPEND L K), therefore, we first have to ensure that the simplest case is catered for. That is, what happens when one of the two list arguments is NIL? The answer is that APPEND must simply return the other. Thus, the APPEND starts with an expression such as:

```
(COND ((NULL L) K))
```

This will return K if L is NIL. Thus we have defined APPEND for the case where its first argument is NIL. We now have to define it for the first argument equal to L. To do this, we assume that it works for lists with one less member than L, and use this somehow to define it for L. At this point we are at liberty to assume that we have:

```
(APPEND (CDR L) K)
```

working perfectly, because (CDR L) is simply an example of a list with one less member than L itself.

Now we have to define specifically how to convert this into working on L itself. The answer comes from the fact that this last expression is only short of the final list by the CAR of L. Think about it before continuing, this is crucial. Draw a picture if you have to!

Thus, the following will produce the final result:

```
(CONS (CAR L) (APPEND (CDR L K)))
```

You can think of this as using CONS to convert the penultimate iteration of the induction into the final iteration.

The question now is how to use the above statements to produce a recursion, and how does the actual iteration which we need to build up the APPEND work?

Recursive definition of APPEND

We have now produced two statements; they were the case where L is NIL, and the last statement above. These are alternatives in the definition of APPEND, and they should thus be placed within a COND as follows:

```
(DEFUN APPEND (L K)
     (COND ((NULL L) K)
               (T (CONS (CAR L) (APPEND (CDR L) K))))))
```

This is actually a full definition of APPEND, and if you type it in and try it out it will work – believe it or not.

You can actually build up all your recursive definitions of functions by thinking of induction in this way. It is important for you to be able to think up the details of a recursive definition for yourself. You will see, shortly, that it is not too difficult to understand how the above works; the main difficulty is how to think of it from the beginning. The induction should give you a clue each time, and we will look at some examples from this point of view.

How APPEND works

This is where you will see that the inductive definition above tricks the computer into performing an entire iteration of APPEND, starting with

NIL and K. Once you call the APPEND function, the computer cannot help itself but loop until L is NIL, when it leaves the definition. The reason for this is simply due to APPEND's call to itself in the last line of its definition.

To understand the actual process which occurs, we will look at some examples of the use of APPEND, and follow them through. To do this, we will rewrite APPEND in a form which makes the exact position of the local variables, L and K, apparent:

```
(DEFUN APPEND (ARG1 ARG2)
    (COND ((NULL ARG1) ARG2)
          (T (CONS (CAR ARG1) (APPEND (CDR ARG1) ARG2))))))
```

Now suppose we use the function in the following examples:

(a) (APPEND () '(A B C))
To evaluate this, LISP looks at the definition of APPEND, and sees that ARG1 is NIL. The first line of its definition says to return ARG2 as the value immediately. Thus the value returned is (A B C), because the first argument is NIL.

(b) (APPEND '(X) '(A B C)
Figure 5.1 shows a slightly different flowchart from normal which is aimed at explaining how this evaluation works.

LISP matches the above pattern with the finished definition, as usual, and sets ARG1 to (X), and ARG2 to (A B C), as shown in the flowchart. LISP then looks at APPEND, and checks to see if ARG1 is NULL, which is not so, and so it proceeds to the rest of the definition of APPEND.

It then finds the CONS function, and has two jobs to do at that point. It has to evaluate the CAR of (X), which is easy, and it has to use APPEND again. These tasks are shown by two arrows coming from this box in the flowchart.

The use of APPEND entails setting APPEND's arguments to (CDR ARG1) and ARG2, as shown. The former is NIL, and the latter is (A B C). Thus APPEND is called with these arguments, and as the first argument is NIL, it simply returns its second argument, and finishes here.

Meanwhile, the CONS has been held up pending the outcome of the two arrows coming out of its flowchart box. At this point, the process returns to the CONS, whose arguments have now been found as X and (A B C), and evaluates it. This gives (X A B C) which is the expected value for the APPEND of (X) and (A B C).

You can see how the CONS part of APPEND is held over, or suspended, until the 'inner' APPEND has been performed – we say that the inner APPEND is at one level down from the outer APPEND. There are, effectively, two iterations of APPEND in this example,

(c) (APPEND '(X Y Z) '(A B C))
Figure 5.2 shows this example being processed so that you can see the iteration proceeding. Follow the solid lines on the way down, and the dotted

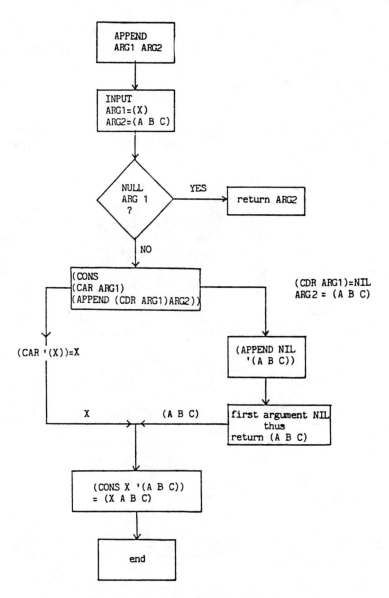

Fig. 5.1 Recursive iteration of APPEND

lines on the way up. Figure 5.1 is used each time an APPEND is reached.

The process starts by placing the arguments above into the APPEND definition, which means calling Figure 5.1.

The difference between this example and the last comes when you reach the first CONS in Figure 5.1. The left-hand arrow from the CONS box is (CAR '(X Y Z)) this time, and it still gives X, which hangs around waiting to be used later. But, the second level call to APPEND, following the right-hand arrow in Figure 5.1, does not give NIL in its first argument. This first argument is (CDR ARG1), and here it is (Y Z). This causes APPEND to be called, at the second level, as:

    (APPEND '(Y Z) '(A B C))

as shown in Figure 5.2.

Figure 5.1 is used again. When the CONS is reached, the left-hand arrow is (CAR '(Y Z)), by this time, and this gives Y, which hangs around, again, until later. The right-hand arrow gives:

    (APPEND '(Z) '(A B C))

and the process repeats again, at this third level giving Z for later, and a final (fourth level) call to APPEND where the first argument is NIL. Figure 5.1 shows what happens next. (A B C) is returned at this level, and the last deferred CONS is performed. This gives (Z A B C), following the dotted arrows in Figure 5.2, then (Y Z A B C) and finally (X Y Z A B C), as

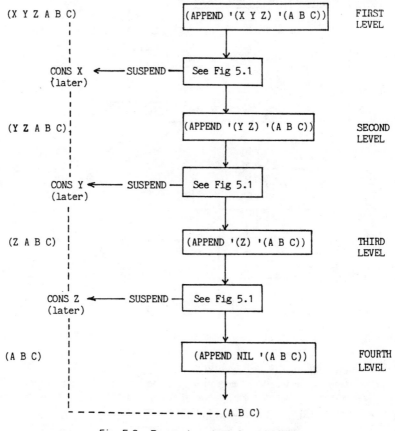

Fig. 5.2 Recursive chart for APPEND

required. The whole process ends here, and the joint list is returned as the function's value.

As you can see, larger lists are treated in exactly the same way, and Figure 5.2 is simply expanded by adding a few more rungs to the ladder. All recursions can be viewed in this manner, and you should keep the picture in mind for all that follows.

Recursion as iteration

There are two types of iteration in this recursion. The first is the repetitive use of Figure 5.1, and the second is the final jump back up the levels, where CONS is iterated to produce the final result. In many ways, the first of these may be viewed as setting up the data for the second. It is the CONS looping which actually performs the build-up of the joint list. In fact, this second iteration is not that different from the definition of APPEND which you were reminded of at the start of this chapter – just turn back and see. In that case, again, single elements were stripped off one of the lists and added to the other. This is one example of a comparison between the use of LOOP and the use of recursion in function definitions. But, there is a far more important comparison which involves neatness and simplicity.

If you look at the LOOP definition of APPEND at the start of this chapter, you would be forgiven for thinking that it is much simpler, and that recursion would seem to be a waste of time from this point of view. Take another look, however, and you see that the LOOP needed CONSR, which was not a LISP function, and that CONSR needed REVERSE which was also not a LISP function. IF you are comparing like with like, the LOOP definition of APPEND would have to be written as follows (see the solutions to Examples 3.5 and 3.6 at the end of Chapter 3):

```
(DEFUN APPEND (L K)
  (LOOP (UNTIL (NULL K) L)
        (SETQ L (CONSR L (CAR K)))
        (SETQ K (CDR K))))

(DEFUN CONSR (L NEW-MEMBER)
  (SETQ L (REVERSE NEW-MEMBER))
  (SETQ L (CONS NEW-MEMBER L))
  (REVERSE L))

(DEFUN REVERSE (L)
  (SETQ REV NIL)
  (LOOP (UNTIL (NULL L) REV)
        (SETQ REV (CONS (CAR L) REV ))
        (SETQ L (CDR L))))
```

It is true that you may be able to find ways of making this whole program neater – but you will have trouble meeting the neatness of the two-line program for the recursive definition of APPEND.

We will now look at several examples of recursion, and produce some useful functions at the same time.

List length - the LEN function

It is often useful to know the length of a list, and we will define LEN for this purpose. LEN simply returns the number of members in its single argument. If its argument is an atom, it gives an error.

To define LEN using loops, we would probably strip off the head of the argument successively, until only NIL was left, and count as we go. The final count would be the length of the argument.

We define LEN similarly using recursion. Remember the inductive method, define it for the simplest case, the singleton here, and then assume it for one less than the length of the argument, and show how you would use this to produce the answer. The first bit is simple:

```
(DEFUN LEN (L)
   (COND ((NULL (CDR L)) 1)
      ( . . . .
```

If L is a singleton, this function will return 1 as its value, because the CDR of a singleton is NIL.

The rest of the definition assumes that LEN works for the CDR of L, and produces the result for L itself from this. Thus, the next part of the definition is something like:

```
(PLUS 1 (LEN (CDR L)))
```

This is all you need, according to the induction argument, and our next job is to put it all together and check that it does the job. The complete definition is:

```
(DEFUN LEN (ARG)
   (COND ((NULL (CDR ARG)) 1)
         (T (PLUS 1 (LEN (CDR ARG)))))))
```

As you know, any variable will do for the local variables of a function, and we have used ARG here to help make the general nature of the argument clear, especially when we see a flowchart for the function's processes.

As you can see, this definition only assumes that the argument is a list, its members can be anything, and whether they are lists, lists of lists, atoms or whatever is irrelevant. You should type this in and check with some general data of your own. To see how it works, Figure 5.3 sketches the process chart for:

```
(LEN '(A B C D))
```

which returns the number 4.

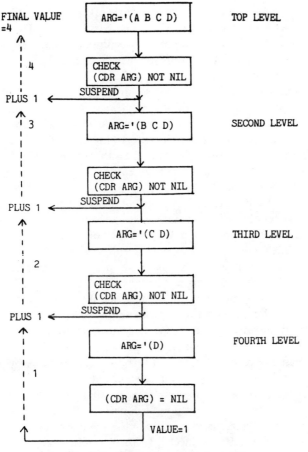

Fig. 5.3 Recursive chart for LEN

Again, follow the solid lines downwards, and the dotted lines on the way up.

ARG is set to (A B C D) at the start, and then its CDR is checked to see if it is empty. As it is not empty, the PLUS 1 is processed, but cannot be performed until the LEN function acting on (CDR ARG) has been evaluated. This causes PLUS 1 to be suspended, and the definition of LEN is used at the second level down. The process is repeated as shown, and the last part occurs when ARG has been reduced to a singleton, and (CDR ARG) is thus NIL. This is when the first part of LEN's definition comes into its own and gives the fourth level call to LEN a definite value, which is 1. The suspended PLUS 1 functions are then performed on this value of LEN, backwards as shown. As you see, this gives the required value of 4.

Example 5.1
(a) Rewrite LEN using LOOP instead of recursion.

(b) Define the function ADDMEM which takes a single list of whole numbers as its argument, and adds the numbers together. The stipulation you may assume is that the total never overflows the limits of your LISP. (c) Define the TIMESMEM function which is exactly as for (b), but multiplies all the numbers instead.

By the time you have done these examples, you should be feeling fairly confident about recursion. It should be clear to you, for instance, that a recursion always has a 'get-out' clause, which lower and lower levels of function calls are continuously striving for. This 'get-out' is the first part of the induction – the bit that looks for the simplest case. This is the main reason for including the simple case – to ensure that the recursion iteration always comes to an end.

It should also be clear to you that one of the tasks of a recursive language interpreter is to allow for memory space somewhere to store all those intermediate levels of processing. We have seen only very simple suspended operations, but no computer can store even these forever. Every machine has a maximum number of recursions it can perform in any situation, though for large machines this can be very great. However, if you write a large recursion on a micro, do not be surprised if you run out of memory. One way out of this is simply to do away with the recursion, and use loops. A loop generally stores very little suspended information; things are usually done immediately as they come up in the loop.

As you can see, recursion is only a form of iteration where you do not specify the loop specifically – it is implied or 'implicit' within the function definition. Some efficient interpreters, or compilers, are capable of recognising cases where a simple loop will perform the same task, and they effectively rewrite the recursion as a loop to save space. This is sometimes called 'tail recursion'. If you meet a LISP or another language with this facility, you should read the manual to see how to activate the facility by writing the recursion in a particular way.

Our next task is to look at some further examples of functions, defined recursively, which you will find very useful in general, if your LISP does not have them already. The first of these is the long promised EQUAL function for general lists.

The EQUAL function

EQ gives the value T if comparing two equal atoms, but apparently equal lists give NIL as the answer. We will now see how to redefine EQ as the function:

```
(EQUAL L K)
```

which is the same as EQ, except that it also gives the value T if its arguments are lists containing lexically equal members. Look back at the definition of EQ if you have forgotten all this, before reading on.

In other words, the following all have the value T:

```
(EQUAL 'A 'A)
(EQUAL '(A B C) '(A B C))
(EQUAL '(A (B C (D E))) '(A (B C (D E))))
```

whereas, for instance, the following has the value NIL:

```
(EQ '(A B C) '(A B C))
```

As usual, the basis of the recursive definition of EQUAL comes from induction. Think of building up the definition, starting off by checking the simplest type of case – i.e. the case where L and K are atoms. This case will be used to finish a recursion which strips the arguments down until they are actually single atoms. The atomic case is covered by EQ. Thus, the definition might start:

```
(DEFUN EQUAL (ARG1 ARG2)
    (COND ((EQ ARG1 ARG2) T)
        (  . . . .
```

This returns the value T if the arguments are EQ, no matter what else you put into the COND list.

The next step is to imagine the next level of complexity which can exist – i.e. just one of the arguments could be an atom, and the other could be a list. In this case, EQUAL should return NIL, because the arguments cannot possibly be equal. This means that the next line in the COND should check for this possibility:

```
(DEFUN EQUAL (ARG1 ARG2)
    (COND   ((EQ ARG1 ARG2) T)
            ((OR (ATOM ARG1) (ATOM ARG2)) NIL)
            (  . . . . . .
```

This second expression will only be reached if the arguments are not equal atoms. If, in this second expression, one of the arguments is an atom, either they are both atoms but different, or just one is an atom. Either way, it is the duty of this expression to return NIL to the function.

This only leaves the case where both arguments are lists. If the processing makes it past the first two expressions, you know you are only dealing with lists, and so you can use list processing functions without risking errors.

We now use the second part of induction by assuming that EQUAL works for parts of ARG1 and ARG2, and use this to check the whole of these arguments. In other words, we break the arguments into pieces, and work on those pieces to build up the complete check. The function EQUAL should return T if the CARs and the CDRs of its arguments are EQUAL. That is, if the following is T:

```
(AND (EQUAL (CAR ARG1) (CAR ARG2))
     (EQUAL (CDR ARG1) (CDR ARG2)))
```

We have to use EQUAL even for the CARs because the CAR of a list may be a sublist, and EQ will not work on this in general.

To see that this completes the definition, imagine two lists being compared. They are first checked as atoms, and then assumed to be lists, and passed to the last expression above. If the CARs of the lists are atoms which are not equal, then the first part is not T, and the AND returns NIL, and the whole function ends. Otherwise, the EQUAL function is called and the evaluation of AND suspended until later. EQUAL may then be called several times again, reducing the arguments down and down until they can be checked as atoms, when EQUAL can make a firm decision, and the backtracking in the recursion occurs.

The process, in fact, eventually checks the equality of every single atom in the arguments. This includes all the atoms in all the sublists of all the sublists etc., etc. This could produce a complexity of suspended operations which would be difficult to contemplate. However, it is all taken care of automatically by the recursion. Now imagine trying to define a loop to perform this complexity of analysis – going into all the sublists of sublists. It is possible, but would be on a very different level of complexity from the definition of EQUAL given below. This is one of the most powerful reasons for including recursion in a programming language.

The function definition for EQUAL is:

```
(DEFUN EQUAL (L K)
    (COND ((EQ L K) T)
          ((OR (ATOM L) (ATOM K)) NIL)
          (T (AND (EQUAL (CAR L) (CAR K))
                  (EQUAL (CDR L) (CDR K)))))))
```

CONSR

In Chapter 3, we defined CONSR, which adds an atom to the end of a list, using REVERSE. We will now see a recursive definition which uses only standard LISP functions. Refresh your memory, if necessary, by looking back at Chapter 3.

Induction tells us to consider the simplest case, and we shall start this time with the empty list:

```
(DEFUN CONSR (L NEW-MEMBER)
    (COND ((NULL L) (LIST NEW-MEMBER))
          ( . . . .
```

where L is a list, and NEW-MEMBER is an atom or a list. For instance, if this is applied as:

```
(CONSR NIL '(A B C))
```

the outcome would be:

```
(LIST '(A B C))
```

which has value:

`((A B C))`

This is a singleton list with a list as its only member – hence the double brackets. This is certainly the correct outcome for the definition of CONSR, and the next step is to assume that it works for the CDR of L, and see how to extend it. The following does this:

`(CONS (CAR L) (CONSR (CDR L) NEW-MEMBER))`

This starts by adding NEW-MEMBER onto the end of CDR of L, and then puts the head of L on, which produces the final answer, once the CONSR part has been done.

You should always check that the recursion ends properly – just as you always have to with loops. Here, the last call to CONSR occurs when L has been reduced to a singleton, of any type. The CDR of L is then NIL, and the expression above asks for (CONSR NIL NEW-MEMBER) which works because of the first expression in CONSR's definition. Thus the recursion is correct – the next step should actually be to test the function. The full definition is:

```
(DEFUN CONSR (L NEW-MEMBER)
   (COND ((NULL L) (LIST NEW-MEMBER))
         (T (CONS (CAR L) (CONSR (CDR L) NEW-MEMBER)))))
```

which is a remarkably neat, and somewhat more satisfying definition than the previous one – it relies on nothing new, and is quite short. It will work with lists containing any complexity of list, and will CONSR anything onto the end.

DELETE

We saw the definition of a restricted version of DELETE defined in Chapter 4 called DEL. It was used as:

`(DEL MEMBER L)`

where MEMBER could only be an atom, and L could only be a non-empty list. DEL also used a non-local variable, which means that the variable must not be in use elsewhere when DEL is called, because its value will be overwritten. The following shows you how to define a new function with none of these disadvantages.

What we really need in AI is a range of DELETE functions. One of them deletes the first occurrence of any kind of member of a list, and the second deletes all the occurrences of that member from the list. Other types of delete will delete any given number of occurrences of the given object. We will stick to the first two and call them DELETE1 and DELETEALL.

The functions should also not give an error if presented with the empty list – they should just return NIL as expected. In addition, the member to be deleted should be able to be any kind of list or atom. In Chapter 4, it was mentioned that DELETE needed a definition of EQUAL – unless your LISP already had this. We will assume in the following that EQUAL has been defined.

To define DELETE1 recursively, the start, as always, is to define the function for the lowest case. This is simply the case where L is NIL. This is achieved as follows:

```
(DEFUN DELETE1 (MEMBER L)
  (COND ((NULL L) NIL)
        ( . . . .
```

This ensures that when DELETE1 is presented with an empty L, the function simply returns NIL for any given MEMBER. This is not really the simplest case of an iteration procedure, so let us consider how the iteration should go, and then look at the simplest case. The iteration has to build up a list from L which takes each member one by one, and checks to see if it is EQUAL to MEMBER. If it is, we simply do not bother to add it to the list we are building up. The simplest case of this is when the CAR of L is MEMBER, and we can return the CDR of L as the final answer.

This adds another expression to the definition, as follows:

```
(DEFUN DELETE1 (MEMBER L)
  (COND ((NULL L) NIL)
        ((EQUAL (CAR L) MEMBER) (CDR L))
        ( . . . . .
```

Thus the recursive iteration is to be performed until this latter situation arises, and the function finishes leaving out the first occurrence of MEMBER.

If the function manages to pass the first two tests without finishing, we know that the L is not NIL, and that its CAR is not MEMBER. We now assume that DELETE1 works for the CDR of L, as usual, and we know it is safe to add the CAR of L onto this to produce the final list. The definition is as follows:

```
(DEFUN DELETE1 (MEMBER L)
  (COND ((NULL L) NIL)
        ((EQUAL (CAR L) MEMBER) (CDR L))
        (T (CONS (CAR L) (DELETE1 MEMBER (CDR L))))))
```

Try this out with some lists, to gain a feel for this function. It is very useful in list processing.

Example 5.2
Define the function DELETEALL which removes all occurrences of MEMBER from L. The clue is that the definition is the same, but you will have to include a second recursive call to the function at one particular point. Can you see where?

Summary

ITERATION is the repetitive processing of a set of expressions. *LOOP* is the normal iterative processing function, recursion is another.

INDUCTION is a process which starts by proving or defining a function for the simplest case in a series and then assuming it for a general case. This is then used to prove or define the function for the next case in the series.

RECURSION is the use of a function within its own definition. The process of induction is used to set up recursive procedures. When the computer finds a recursive definition, it cannot help iterating through the process. It is important to ensure that the process comes to an end by defining the simplest case correctly.

Solutions to problems

Example 5.1

(a) LEN can be defined by adding 1 to a counter with each loop, as the head of the given list is stripped off. The process finishes when the list is reduced to NIL. A possible definition is:

```
(DEFUN LEN (L)
  (SETQ COUNT 0)
  (LOOP (UNTIL (NULL L) COUNT)
        (SETQ L (CDR L))
        (SETQ COUNT (PLUS 1 COUNT)))))
```

(b) ADDMEM is defined recursively by considering induction, as usual. Build the definition up from a singleton list – the single member is actually the answer. Thus, the first step in the definition would be to examine the CDR of the given list, see if it is empty, and if it is then the CAR of the given list is the answer. ADDMEM starts as follows:

```
(DEFUN ADDMEM (L)
  (COND ((NULL (CDR L)) (CAR L))
        ( . . . .
```

The next step is to assume that you have ADDMEM for the list just below the one given, and write out a method of extending this to give the answer. The method is almost the same as for LEN, except that instead of adding 1 to the LEN of the CDR, we add the actual value of the CAR of L to the ADDMEM of the CDR of L. This gives the following full definition:

```
(DEFUN ADDMEM (L)
  (COND ((NULL (CDR L)) (CAR L))
        (T (PLUS (CAR L) (ADDMEM (CDR L))))))
```

You should type this in, check it, and then draw a process chart for it – this will help you in constructing future recursions.

(c) TIMESMEM is very similar in structure to the previous examples. Again, the first part deals with singletons, and then TIMESMEM itself is used to convert the multiple of the CDR elements into the final answer by multiplying by the CAR element. The definition is:

```
(DEFUN TIMESMEM (L)
    (COND ((NULL (CDR L)) (CAR L))
          (T (TIMES (CAR L) (TIMESMEM (CDR L))))))
```

Again, you should try it out, and quickly sketch the chart.

Example 5.2

The function DELETEALL gives us an example of a double recursion. There is no reason why a given function definition should not include as many recursion procedures in it as you wish – just as you can have many separate loops within a program.

To change DELETE1 to remove every occurrence of MEMBER, have a careful look at the second expression in the definition of DELETE1. This is where the recursion finishes with the list having been whittled down until MEMBER is exposed at the head of the list. DELETE1 ends here leaving any other MEMBERs in the CDR of the list.

It would be so nice if that CDR could also be rid of all of its MEMBERs, to produce an answer to DELETEALL. This can be arranged with the greatest of ease using the magic of recursion – simply DELETEALL MEMBERs from it. Unbelievable? Look at the following definition of DELETEALL and see for yourself:

```
(DEFUN DELETEALL (MEMBER L)
   (COND ((NULL L) NIL)
         ((EQUAL (CAR L) MEMBER)(DELETEALL MEMBER (CDR L)))
         (T (CONS (CAR L) (DELETEALL MEMBER (CDR L))))))
```

Here, when the main recursion finishes, a new recursion opens up to remove all the MEMBERS from CDR of L.

Chapter Six
More Advanced Uses of Functions

Introduction

We have now seen all the major parts of LISP, and you should have tried a fair number of examples. We will look in this chapter at some advances on the basic facilities which LISP functions can offer. For instance, there are several types of function which exist as standard functions, but you would not be able to write them for yourself with the information given so far.

This book is generally introductory, and the information in this chapter effectively leads you on to the next stage by introducing the more complex concepts which are used in LISP. It is most important that you keep your LISP manual handy because as we delve deeper into functions, we enter a realm where almost everything is defined slightly differently from dialect to dialect. The differences should be small, and the principles are the same, but check carefully as you go.

The chapter starts by introducing some new ways of looking at functions in general, and then defines the last few generally available LISP functions.

Functions in general

Functions are not always confined to being defined as a list of arguments and expressions in a DEFUN statement. It is possible, for instance, to form functions as the results of other calculations. After all, a function definition is just a list with a specific form, and lists can be built up by list building functions. The argument list of a function can also be formed in this way.

We cannot fully explore these advanced concepts here, but the following sections give you some of the essential background which will help when you meet these ideas in advanced books on LISP.

One of the simpler concepts to explain is the one of a list building operation which ends up with a list of items which have to be used as arguments of another function. For instance, suppose you were to define a function which always gives a list containing two numbers as its returned value, and the final operation you wish to be performed is to add the numbers together.

To see the problem, imagine how you would do this. The function which gives the list of two numbers might return the list (5 6) bound to the identifier L. You cannot simply use:

```
(PLUS L)
```

or something similar, because PLUS takes two arguments – each of them with a numeric value. You first have to extract the numbers from L, and then apply PLUS to them. Thus you might use:

```
(PLUS (CAR L) (CADR L))
```

which works perfectly well. However, suppose the first function actually returned a list of an unknown number of numbers, and your next job was to sum the numbers in this list of arbitrary length. Suppose also, for the sake of this example, that PLUS could take an arbitrary number of arguments, and simply sum them. How would you apply PLUS to the list of numbers? PLUS has to appear at the head of the list containing its arguments in the tail, so how would you strip off the elements of the numeric list, and place them in a list with PLUS at its head?

The APPLY function

The answer to the last question is that you do not have to; there is usually a function called APPLY which saves you the bother.

Please do check your own LISP manual before continuing because it is likely that APPLY is written in a slightly different manner to that given below. It is generally the case that the more advanced the feature being discussed, the more dialect-specific it is likely to be.

The way APPLY works is simply to apply any function to the elements of a given list as if they were extracted and fed to the function in the normal way. For instance:

```
(APPLY PLUS L)
```

would give the value 11 if L was bound to (5 6). If PLUS works for multiple arguments, the above expression will work for any sized list, and simply sum the elements, all of which have to be numbers. This is exactly the same as ADDMEM in Example 5.1(b), but is considerably neater. You can do the same for TIMESMEM too.

Note that some LISPs insist that you put a QUOTE before the function name in the above. Once again, check your LISP carefully.

APPLY is thus generally used to apply a function to a list whose elements form a valid argument list for that function.

Other examples are:

```
If L = (A B)  then (APPLY CONS L) = (A.B)

If L = (A (A B C A)) then (APPLY DELETEALL A L) = (B C)
```

To understand the latter, remember that DELETEALL takes two arguments – the first of which is removed from the list in the second.

APPLY is very useful in the situation where you are manipulating lists in general, and you find you have a list whose members are set up perfectly for the next operation, but they are locked up within round brackets. APPLY allows you to leave the members where they are while a function acts'on them. Later we will see a function which goes even further in applying functions to members of a list.

A general function definition – LAMBDA

When you define a function, the definition is generally held as a list of defining expressions, bound by a memory pointer to the function name. This implies that the function definition has something of a separate existence, in a certain sense, to the function's identifier. This is in fact the case. Indeed, you can define a function without actually specifying an identifier. Of course, it is not possible actually to store that definition in isolation in such a form, unless it is bound to a function name. However, this can be very useful, as well as telling you a little more about the structure of LISP.

If you type in a LISP standard function, without its customary brackets and identifiers, and press RETURN, or whatever, you will probably know by now that the machine prints something like:

SUBR followed by a number

The exact response depends upon your LISP. This is a method of informing you that the function name you have typed in is bound to a machine code routine which you cannot inspect. If, on the other hand, you type in the name of a function which is defined in LISP expressions, such as your own functions, the response will normally be to print up the complete function definition prefaced by the word LAMBDA, and not by the function name itself.

For instance, if you have the recursive definition of LEN stored in the computer, and you then type in the word LEN on its own, you should expect to see something like:

```
(LAMBDA (ARG) (COND ((NULL
(CDR ARG)) 1) (T (PLUS 1 (
LEN (CDR ARG))))))
```

depending upon the line length which your display shows. LISP has, as usual, tried to evaluate your input, and uses LEN to find a value bound to it. The value bound to a function definition is simply the list which you typed in using DEFUN followed by the function name.

You can see that the definition is simply printed out in a long line, which overflows as necessary. No function name is used – just the general function header which is called LAMBDA. Every function you print out in this way will be headed by LAMBDA, and the binding to the function name is not mentioned specifically. This is true of some editors too, and one such package is described in Appendix 2. The function is always called up by name, but it is printed out in this general manner.

LAMBDA is essentially a method of signalling that what follows is a list which is to be taken as a function definition. By now you should have the definite feeling that a function without a function name is rather useless. However, there is a very powerful use of this type of general function definition which concerns the concept of using functions as arguments of other functions. The next section takes this further.

The mapping function MAPC

Please note once again that what follows is slightly dialect-dependent, though of course the principles will be the same. There is also more than one 'mapping function' included with most LISPs, but we shall look at just one here.

In an analogous manner to APPLY, it is often necessary to be able to apply a function definition to every member of a general list, and produce the answers in a new list.

For instance, suppose you were given a list L of the form:

```
((Peter loves Janet)
 (Paul loves Mary)
 (John loves Rosemary)
 (George . . . . . . . .
```

which is of arbitrary length, and perhaps has been formed from a repetitive read, or an analysis of a set of sentences. To produce a list of all the boys' names from this list requires the CARs of all the elements in the list, and CADDRs for the girls. To form these two lists, we could do with a way of applying CAR and CADDR to each member of the list in turn. This is called mapping, and the function MAPC does it. The two required lists would be:

```
BOYS = (MAPC CAR L)   and GIRLS = (MAPC CADDR L)
```

You should type this is in to try it, and then try to produce an expression which gives the three verbs in a list – i.e. (loves loves loves).

You should now be able to see the difference between APPLY and MAPC. APPLY takes a list whose members form the normal argument set for the function being applied, while MAPC applies the given function to each member of the list as if it were the single argument of the mapped function.

To see how LAMBDA comes into all of this, it is possible to replace CAR and CADDR above by a LAMBDA list. For instance, consider the unbound function definition:

```
(LAMBDA (X) (TIMES 3 X))
```

This function trebles any single number it is given. To treble all the members of a given list, L, simply use this LAMBDA expression after the MAPC:

```
(MAPC '(LAMBDA (X) (TIMES 3 X)) L)
```

Notice that the LAMBDA expression is QUOTEd here – this is always necessary when using a LAMBDA expression. The MAPC here simply applies the LAMBDA definition of the treble function to each member of L, stores the answers in a new list, and returns this new list as the value of MAPC.

The fact that the LAMBDA is quoted should suggest something about the first argument of MAPC.

Before MAPC can apply its first argument to its second, they both have to be evaluated. The first argument must turn out to have a value which is a function definition, or MAPC will fail. There are three ways in which the first argument can have a function definition as its value. First, it could be a normal function identifier. Second, it could be an actual list containing a function definition, which means a LAMBDA expression. The third method would be for another function to produce a variable with a list stored in it which turned out to be a LAMBDA expression.

By the last method, you should be able to envisage a situation where a LISP program produces an output which is another LISP program, made up of function definitions stored in variables. A case of computers programming themselves – or Artificial Intelligence at its most threatening!

More general types of function

If you consider some of the standard LISP functions, and then compare their facilities with the ones you can produce using DEFUN, you will see that there are a few things missing. For instance, functions such as LIST can take an arbitrary number of arguments. So far you have only been shown how to specify the exact number of arguments required using DEFUN. Also, there are functions such as SETQ which do not evaluate all of their arguments, but consider them as if they had been QUOTEd. There are functions such as SETQ and RPLACA which actually alter the values of one of their arguments, as well as returning a value as usual. Finally, it is useful to be able to use more local variables than just the arguments declared in the DEFUN. This saves altering values which may be in use by an outer function.

None of these facilities has been explained for your own use yet, and as with most advanced functional uses, the method of dealing with the points is, once again, dialect-dependent. For instance, some LISPs actually use names other than DEFUN for defining special types of function, and some use a special function called PROG for a number of special facilities. The following gives a common way in which DEFUN is used, but you will have to read your LISP manual with care to ensure that what follows is in keeping with your dialect.

Functions with multiple and unevaluated arguments

A common way in which LISPs provide for multiple and unevaluated arguments is to allow the list of arguments in DEFUN to be replaced by a single non-NIL identifier which will become bound to a list of arguments when the function is called up. For instance, suppose you wish to define a function called FN1 which can take any number of arguments, and does not evaluate any of its arguments. The way to do this is to start the definition as:

```
(DEFUN FN1 ARGS
    ( . . . . .
```

The list of arguments is replaced by the single identifier ARGS. When the function is used, no QUOTEs are required on the arguments. The function could be called up as:

```
(FN1 A B C D E F)
```

The arguments shown are taken literally, as if QUOTEd, and combined into a list by LISP, and bound to ARGS. Thus ARGS now equals (A B C D E F). To use the arguments in the function body, CAR and CDR have to be used to separate them out.

As an example, suppose you need a function called CHTOTAL which adds up the number of characters in a sentence, and suppose the sentence was to be given to the function as separate words, without any QUOTEs – i.e. the arguments are not evaluated. It would work as follows:

```
(CHTOTAL How many letters are there in this)
```

This would return the number of letters, without spaces, as 28. The way in which it would be defined would be to look at each argument separately, by stripping off the head of ARGS, EXPLODEing it, using the LEN function to find its length, and then adding all of these up. This can be done in a loop as follows:

```
(DEFUN CHTOTAL ARGS
    (SETQ N 0)
    (LOOP (UNTIL (NULL ARGS) N)
          (SETQ N (PLUS N (LEN (EXPLODE (CAR ARGS)))))
          (SETQ ARGS (CDR ARGS))))
```

As you can see, the single identifier ARGS has been bound to a list containing the arguments as given, without evaluating them. N is used to accumulate the total, and is not local. It is started from 0. If ARGS is empty, then the first expression in the loop ends the process, and the answer is 0.

Note that the function body does not use arguments in the same way as in the usual DEFUN use, instead it uses parts of the list ARGS, which it has to find by CAR and CDR.

The next part of the loop increases N by the length of the first member of ARGS exploded. ARGS is then reduced to its CDR, and the next time the loop passes, it is the length of the head of this reduced list which is added to N.

Example 6.1
How would you set about to define CHTOTAL using recursion instead of a loop and a non-local variable – and would it work?

Evaluating the arguments

Using the above, a function can have any number of arguments, but they are not evaluated. This can be a problem, however, and in general you will want at least some of them to be evaluated, so that other functions can pass values to that function as variable values. To evaluate some or all of the arguments, you must use the EVAL function. Thus variables can be placed as arguments in the function call, and the function definition can do the evaluating of some or all of those arguments.

An example of this would be a function which perhaps had a single variable in its first place, and any number of literal arguments following. The function might be defined as:

```
(DEFUN FN2 ARGS
    (SETQ X (PLUS 8 (EVAL (CAR ARGS))))
    ( . . . . .
```

When FN2 is used, with a number of arguments, the start of this function treats the first argument supplied as a variable, and finds its value. It then adds 8 to the value, and stores it in the variable X. The remaining arguments are called up and used as literals; they are not evaluated. It is important, of course, that the function is used correctly, and that the first argument has the correct item placed in it.

Further local variables

The definition of local variables within a function definition, other than the normal arguments, is almost entirely dialect-specific.

Some LISPs define a function called PROG which is used within the body of the definition and whose arguments are local to that definition.

Acornsoft LISP uses a method of signifying extra arguments in the DEFUN which do not have to be used in the function call, but are nevertheless local. This is done by placing these extra arguments at the end of the normal argument list and each one enclosed within brackets. For instance, the following has two normal arguments, and two optional arguments – i.e., a function call may include or omit the latter. Either way, they are local variables:

```
(DEFUN FN3 (X Y (Z) (T))
    (. . . . . .
```

X and Y must be included when the function is called up, but Z and T are not necessary, and they are still local. This allows you to use extra variables within the function definition, without affecting their values which may be in use in the calling program.

Functions which change their arguments' values

SETQ, RPLACA and RPLACD all actually change the value of one of their given arguments.

Consider the following function definition:

```
(DEFUN ADD (X Y Z)
    (SET X (PLUS Y Z)))
```

This is a normal function definition, and simply adds the last two arguments, and places the value in the first, in some way. When the ADD is called, its second two arguments contain numbers, but the first argument is supposed to contain an identifier. However, that identifier must be QUOTEd to ensure that it is the identifier itself, and not its value, which is passed to the function definition. For instance:

```
(ADD 'G 6 7)
```

will match the identifier G up with X, 6 with Y and 7 with Z. That is, within the function, X has the value G. The SET then evaluates X, to give G, and sets that value to 13. Thus G itself is set to 13. As G is not a local variable, because it is not declared as an argument in the DEFUN, its value is retained when the function finishes. You can see that SET was needed, and not SETQ, as it was important actually to evaluate its first argument.

This gives an example of a function which changes the value of an argument. However, it should be possible to define the function so that the identifier does not have to be QUOTEd.

This can be done by defining the function as a function which does not evaluate its first argument. The actual identifier which is placed in that spot when the function is called can be used in a SET within the function body.

As above, the value will be changed externally as it is not a local variable. SET is needed, and not SETQ, for the same reason as above.

As an example, we will redefine the ADD function above to allow the first to be an unQUOTEd identifier. It is defined as:

```
(DEFUN ADD ARGS
     (SET (CAR ARGS) (PLUS (CADR ARGS) (CADDR ARGS))))
```

When the function is called up as:

```
(ADD G 6 7)
```

LISP starts by setting ARGS to the list (G 6 7). The function definition then SETs the CAR of this list to the sum of the other two members using CADR and CADDR to find the other arguments.

In short, this sets G to 13, and leaves the value in G when the function finishes.

Example 6.2

Define the following function. MULTIPLY sets the identifier in its first argument equal to the product of the rest of its arguments. All arguments are to be evaluated.

As a clue, use TIMESMEM from a previous example, but modify it to evaluate the members of the list it acts on.

Summary

APPLY. This function takes two arguments, the first of which is a function, and the second a list. The APPLY function applies the given function to the list as if the list contained an applicable set of arguments for that function. *LAMBDA* allows you to write out a function definition for immediate use, without having to name it. This is also the method used to store function definitions in LISP, usually with a pointer to a function name.

MAPC. This function takes a function followed by a list as its arguments. The function is applied to each member of the list as if that member were the required argument for the given function. The returned value is a list containing the values from the given function being applied to each member of the given list.

Multiple unevaluated arguments. A function can take an arbitrary number of arguments, none of which is evaluated unless specifically done so in the function definition. In the LISP described above, this is achieved by replacing the normal argument list in DEFUN by a single identifier which is bound to a list containing all the arguments used when the function is called. The separate arguments are extracted from this identifier using normal list manipulation functions.

Extra local variables. It is useful to be able to define extra local variables within a function for such uses as a loop counter without affecting the state of external variables which may be in use by other functions. The method of defining further local variables is entirely dependent upon your own LISP. *Changing the values of given arguments.* Functions such as SETQ change the value of an external variable which is supplied as an argument. This can be achieved by defining a function so as to allow the first argument, for instance, to be evaluated which should yield an identifier if the function has been called correctly. The function definition can then be used to set that identifier to some value. The value of that identifier will then be available externally.

Solutions to problems

Example 6.1
To define CHTOTAL recursively, you would start by defining its action on the simplest case, which is the case where ARGS contains a single word. We will discount function calls where the argument is empty.

The simplest case would thus start the definition off as:

```
(DEFUN CHTOTAL ARGS
       (COND ((NULL (CDR ARGS)) (LEN (EXPLODE (CAR ARGS))))
             ( .  .  .  .  .
```

This returns the correct number for a call of the form:

```
(CHTOTAL Hello)
```

which would have the value 5.

The next part of the recursion would be to assume that CHTOTAL works on the CDR of ARGS, and add in the extra number from the CAR of ARGS. This should give an expression of the form:

```
(PLUS (LEN (EXPLODE (CAR ARGS))) (CHTOTAL (CDR ARGS)))
```

This should add the character length of the head member of ARGS to the total number of characters in the tail. Can you see what happens?

EVAL will have no trouble with the first argument of PLUS, but the second argument will not work. The problem is due to the fact that CHTOTAL does not evaluate its arguments, it takes them literally. It tries to find at least one identifier, and here it is followed by a collection of characters which starts with a left bracket. This is not an identifier, by definition, and the function gives an error. It will not evaluate (CDR ARGS) to produce the desired list.

If CHTOTAL is not allowed to evaluate its arguments, it cannot be used in recursion as above.

Example 6.2

MULTIPLY must take any number of arguments, and evaluate them all. In particular, its first argument is evaluated to be an identifier which is subsequently set to the outcome of a calculation, and the definition starts off as:

```
(DEFUN MULTIPLY ARGS
    (SET (CAR ARGS) ( . . . . .
```

The second argument of the SET above has to return the product of the rest of the members of (CDR ARGS). This can be done using a modified form of TIMESMEM defined in Example 5.1. This modified form evaluates the members of the list it is multiplying before using TIMES. We will call the new multiply function TIMESMEMV. Given this, MULTIPLY can be defined as:

```
(DEFUN MULTIPLY ARGS
    (SET (CAR ARGS) (TIMESMEMV (CDR ARGS))))
```

TIMESMEMV automatically evaluates the members of the list as it goes, and this is where MULTIPLY's arguments are evaluated, within the list ARGS.

TIMESMEMV is defined as:

```
(DEFUN TIMESMEMV (L)
    (COND ((NULL (CDR L)) (EVAL (CAR L)))
    (T (TIMES (EVAL (CAR L)) (TIMESMEMV (CDR L))))))
```

The only difference here is that instead of simply working on the members of L, it works on the values of the members of L.

To check MULTIPLY, first of all set a few identifiers to numeric values, and decide on the identifier you want to be set to the product. We will assume that A, B and C have the following values:

$$A = 9 \qquad B = 8 \qquad C = 7$$

and that K is to be set to the product of these numbers. The function would be called as:

(MULTIPLY K A B C)

No quotes are needed, and the result is that K is set to the number 504.

This sort of function would normally be called from another program, and thus performs a given subroutine effectively, and saves having to use SETQ on K to return the required value in K.

The value returned by the function will also be the value of K because the SET is the last function evaluated.

Note that an error will occur if you call MULTIPLY with just one argument.

Chapter Seven
LISP Programming and AI

Introduction

The book so far has been orientated largely towards your learning LISP. If you have worked your way through to this point, you will have an excellent knowledge and feeling for LISP, even if you do not realise it! This chapter looks at a few example programs and shows you how to construct a large program in LISP. If you want to be a LISP programmmer, you should try to extend the programs below for yourself – many of them are open-ended anyway – as well as looking for more applications.

As you should be aware by now, AI has not reached the position where it can give you a prescription for building intelligent machines comparable with humans, but many researchers believe it to be an attainable goal. For the moment, we can only stick to such applications as simple games, natural language analysis, or useful database programs. However, we are slowly investigating the meaning of intelligence in this way. Do not become discouraged by the lack of sophisticatioon of modern AI; there are many corners of the subject which are very advanced. Instead, you should continually analyse and think of those aspects of intelligence which you would like to see mechanised. In this way, you can move towards a definition of intelligence, which is the first step to its understanding and reproduction.

This chapter necessarily uses the ideas and structures defined up to this point in the book, and you should refresh your memory continuously as exactly how to use a given function or expression.

No specific numbered exercises are given here, but you should have a go at defining each function for yourself before reading the definition given, and see if you can produce alternatives which check out on your computer.

You will probably find that an editor will be quite useful in trying out the examples in this chapter, and Appendix 2 describes one for Acornsoft LISP. You may find that the editor with your LISP works similarly. Either way, refer to your manual, as usual.

Classes of example

AI contains a number of apparently diverse areas, and you have seen some of these already. One in particular was the analysis of a data tree, and a simple type of game. This can be taken further – imagine what happens as the tree grows bigger, the number of branches increase from each node, and two branches join up to produce a loop in the tree structure. This last change brings us to the study of networks, or maze-searching programs. The problem is to search a tree, and find a way through from one side to the other. This is a simple problem if the tree has no closed loops – but how do you prevent your program from being stuck forever searching around a closed loop, looking for its end?

Other examples are in the analysis of human language. It is not difficult to write programs which take in a stylised sentence, say three words, and extract the subject, object and verb. These can then be matched up with a vocabulary, and some sort of meaning imparted to the machine for its use in a question and answer program. The problems arise as we allow the sentence to become larger, and more general. How does the machine distinguish between the noun use and the verb use of the word GRATE, for instance? The two meanings are not even related in this case. You may say that context is the answer but try explaining that to a computer program!

The area of expert systems tries to give the human an intelligent aid for looking for information. For instance, the storage of data on motorcycle parts for all the cycles in common use forms a tremendously large bank of data. It is true that searching for a particular part by part number is trivial, but when someone comes into a shop and asks for a part, it is often a general description. The buyer knows what he wants fairly accurately, but certainly not by part number.

It is possible to devise a system which asks questions, and forms the next set of questions as a result of the previous responses. Also, the program can make statistical decisions, and even come out with a solution which might be several parts, each with a probability attached to it. The buyer could then be asked to choose one of these, and bring it back if wrong, or go back to the machine, armed with a couple of intelligent questions to bring back answers to the machine. In this way, the machine would actually suggest those distinguishing features the buyer should look for, in order to make his request specific next time.

A variation on this is the intelligent technical manual. A program could be devised which would ask the user intelligent questions and, depending upon the answers, suggest particular actions to try.

All of the above examples have a common factor – *list manipulation*. The quantity of numerical calculation in these tasks is minimal. The tasks above are different in character from the problem of solving a long and complex equation, or calculating the stresses in a bridge. However, the union of the two types of example yield some very fruitful ideas. For instance, in the case of bridge design, a program could lead the user through the qualitative aspects of the design, and perform the engineering calculations as a background activity to allow him to check his ideas practically. This brings you to the realm of computer-aided design or CAD.

None of the above examples is so complex and esoteric that you cannot begin to see a solution. Think about any one of them, draw the start of a flowchart, and you will find that you can begin right away.

One of the biggest problems that a beginner has in any language is to see how to produce large programs in a structured and well-organised manner. In BASIC, a list processing program to perform comparatively simple tasks can take up dozens or even hundreds of program lines, in one continuous program. It has been said many times in this book that LISP encourages structuring and good organisation in large programs, and the examples below are thus chosen to form a large program for a particular task in order to illustrate how to put together large programs in LISP. The final program also shows a method of employing a learning process. The program is designed to become better and better at its defined task. The task will be an AI application, but first we need a program which will sort a list of numbers into descending order.

Sorting

The need for a sorting program is so universal in list processing that no LISP book is really complete without one. The main reason for describing it here, however, is that it is needed in the application example we will be looking at later.

We have already seen a sort program which acted just on three numbers. It was called TRI-SORT, and you should return to Chapter 3 to refresh your memory, because TRI-SORT will be assumed in the following.

TRI-SORT showed a simple example of a very common sorting method. There are many methods of sorting, and if you are interested in this area, many magazines publish articles on sorting regularly, and many books mention different methods. You only have to read one of the methods, and once you have the idea, simply transfer it into LISP code.

You cannot easily sort letters in LISP, as there is generally no comparison function available, but numbers can be sorted, and if your LISP allows use of ASCII codes, you can sort the letters on these. Later we will be sorting the letters according to some special numeric data, but for now we will stick to numbers only.

The method of sorting in TRI-SORT was to 'bubble' the highest number up to the end of the list, and then work on the other two numbers, or the remainder of the list, and repeat the operation. Of course, with three numbers it is simple, but the principle remains the same with long lists. The highest number is bubbled up to the top of the list, and left where it is for the rest of the program. Then the highest number in the remainder of the list is bubbled up, and this gives two numbers at the end of the list. Again, the routine is repeated on the remainder of the list, and so on. The end result is a sorted list. You can do this operation either way round, and produce lists which are ascending or descending.

For a later example we need a list to be sorted into descending order, and we will write a program for this now.

Descending order sort

The method is to move the smallest number down to the end of the list, and then work on the remainder. Let us assume that the function is called DSORT, and the given list SLIST. SLIST will contain pure numbers, without any sublists.

We will split the operation into two parts. The first part will be the function DSORT, and the second will be a function which DSORT calls, and which we will call STONE. STONE simply takes a list as its argument, and returns the same list with its smallest member moved down to the end of the list.

STONE takes a list as its single argument. It will be defined recursively, and starts by returning the list intact if it is a singleton (see Figure 7.1). Thus STONE starts as:

```
(DEFUN STONE (SLIST)
   (COND ((NULL (CDR SLIST)) SLIST)
         ( . . . . .
```

The next step is to assume that STONE works on lists smaller than SLIST, and use it to STONE the complete list. There are two alternatives to consider. Figure 7.1 shows the process. Consider SLIST to be:

```
(A B C D . . . . . )
```

If the head, A, of SLIST is greater than the next member, then that head cannot be the smallest number in the list, and it is safe to STONE just the CDR and add the head back on later. The following will produce the required answer:

```
(CONS (CAR SLIST) (STONE (CDR SLIST)))
```

If, on the other hand, A is not greater than B, then A might actually be the smallest, and it must not be missed out of the STONE. This can be assured by swopping it with B, which cannot be the smallest, and repeating the above. This time, the following will work:

```
(CONS (CADR SLIST)
      (STONE (CONS (CAR SLIST) (CDDR SLIST))))
```

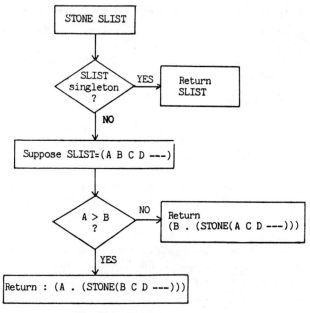

Fig. 7.1 Flowchart for STONE

Here, CADR is used to bring the second element to the head of the list, and STONE is given the CDDR with the CAR CONSed onto it to work on. Just read the above expression through carefully, and check that you understand it before continuing.

The complete definition of STONE is as follows:

```
(DEFUN STONE (SLIST)
  (COND ((NULL (CDR SLIST)) SLIST)
        ((GREATERP (CAR SLIST) (CADR SLIST))
            (CONS (CAR SLIST) (STONE (CDR SLIST))))
        (T (CONS (CADR SLIST)
              (STONE (CONS (CAR SLIST) (CDDR SLIST)))))))
```

Now that we can STONE the smallest number to the end of the list, we can work on one less element next time. However, a quick way to write a sort into ascending order from STONE above is simply to apply STONE to the whole of the given list over and over again. In fact you only have to apply it once less than there are members in the list. To see how this works by example, consider the following set:

(1 2 3)

The first STONE gives:

(2 3 1)

and if STONE is applied again, this becomes:

(3 2 1)

because STONE works by swopping the numbers in pairs just as for TRI-SORT. Thus two applications of STONE to this three-member list sorts it. If you try this on larger lists you will see that the same thing holds. This is highly inefficient, because STONE is made to work on every single list element each time it is called. However, it is given below. For this definition of DSORT, you will need to type in the LEN function:

```
(DEFUN DSORT (SLIST)
    (SETQ N (LEN SLIST))
    (LOOP (UNTIL (EQ N 1) SLIST)
          (SETQ SLIST (STONE SLIST))
          (SETQ N (PLUS N -1)))))
```

This works perfectly, but you should now spend a little time rewriting the loop to allow just the minimum number of STONEs to be performed, for maximum efficiency.

The sort here will be modified for the next example, but will still use this inefficient form.

Code encryption

In order to see an example of building up a long program, we will now look at an application which has a long and interesting history in computing. It is the task of decoding a coded message.

There are many complex ways in which messages can be encoded, or encrypted, and we can only scratch the surface here. The following example is interesting partly because it is a long program, and partly because it gives an excellent example of a learning process. The program will be constructed to allow it to learn how to decode a given type of code, and store its knowledge for later use.

The code involved is simple letter transposition. Each letter of the alphabet is attached to a different coded letter, and the message changed letter by letter into this new format. The code can be cracked easily if you already know the frequencies of all the letters of the alphabet. For instance, E is the most frequent letter in English, and thus if X appears most frequently in the coded message, X is probably equal to E. This does not imply the converse, that E, in code, is equal to X in reality.

To crack a code without knowing the actual prescription used, you will need a reasonably large number of coded messages to use as examples, and infer the code from this. If there are few words to work on, it is difficult to crack the code. However, with a vocabulary bank too, the code cracker can produce a decoded version with some of the letters in the message being either undecoded, or perhaps having several suggestions as to their real value. The vocabulary can then be searched for near matches, and the message may be able to be further decoded.

Other tricks include noting single-letter words which can only be A or I, and three letter words which occur frequently such as THE. Humans can do this very efficiently, and given a partially decoded message, this can be scanned by eye, and probably improved considerably from our own knowledge of both vocabulary and context. The use of context is a rather complex step for automation, but vocabulary scanning is comparatively straightforward.

We will look at two main programs. One will take in as much ordinary text as possible, and gradually learn the letter frequencies in normal words. The other will take in an coded message, and return its version of a decoding. At the same time, the coded message will be used to enable the program to learn a little more about the code.

The decoding will be done purely by counting letter frequencies and matching these to known letter frequencies. Frequencies will be matched by order. For instance, as above, if X is the most common letter, it will be set equal to E; if T is the next most common in the coded message, it will be set to A, or whatever it regards as the next most common letter in English. This is repeated until the message is 'decoded'.

Letter frequency program

This program will learn the frequencies of all the letters of the alphabet as you type in more and more text. The first problem is to decide on how to store the knowledge.

The data which the program produces will be, initially, simply accumulated totals of occurrences of each letter ever encountered. Later this will have to be used to sort the alphabet into relative frequencies, and hence write the alphabet in frequency order.

Once the alphabet is available in frequency order, the coded message can be read into another program, and its letters also placed in frequency order. The two sets can then be compared.

We could store the accumulated frequencies in a number of ways. First, we could produce an association list, with each letter at the head of a list which just contained the accumulated frequency to date as a number in the tail. Second, the data could be stored as a property list. Each letter could have the property ATOTAL attached to it, whose value is the accumulated total so far.

We will choose property lists, because the storage is simple, and they are faster. They come to the same thing in the end.

Figure 7.2 shows a flowchart for a possible program to accumulate frequency data. We will assume that the words are to be input by hand, and this will need a READ expression. There has to be a way of finishing the program, and this can be done by inputing something like XXX, which will not generally occur in normal text. The next step is to EXPLODE the word into individual letters.

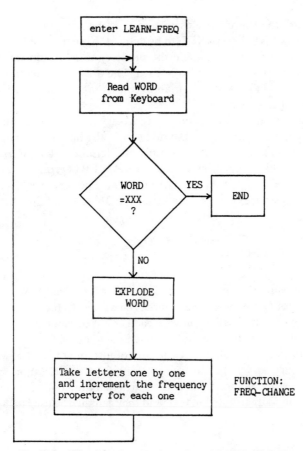

Fig. 7.2 Word frequency learning: LEARN-FREQ

Each letter is then recognised, and the present state of a frequency accumulating property, called something like ATOTAL, is incremented for that letter.

We will call this function LEARN-FREQ. We will also write the function which changes the frequency properties for a given word separately and call it FREQ-CHANGE. This function will be useful when we come to decoding.

LEARN-FREQ is essentially a large loop, and can be defined as follows:

```
(DEFUN LEARN-FREQ ()
    (PRINT '(INPUT WORDS WITH RETURNS))
    (PRINT '(FINISH WITH XXX))
    (PRINT)
    (LOOP (SETQ WORD (READ))
          (UNTIL (EQ WORD 'XXX) 'PROG-ENDS)
          (SETQ WORD (EXPLODE WORD))
          (FREQ-CHANGE 'ATOTAL WORD)))
```

This follows the flowchart closely, and uses the minimum of messages. It now requires FREQ-CHANGE to be defined. Note that FREQ-CHANGE takes two arguments. These are the property to be incremented for each letter, and the exploded word to be used. This allows the function to be used in other contexts with other variables containing the exploded word, and acting on other properties.

At an intermediate stage such as this, when you have a function defined as above but bits are missing, you should type in the function and test it before continuing. This can be done simply by defining FREQ-CHANGE as anything you like, and checking that LEARN-FREQ runs, takes in inputs, explodes words, calls FREQ-CHANGE and does end when you type in XXX. For instance, you could define FREQ-CHANGE, for the moment, as:

```
(DEFUN FREQ-CHANGE (X Y)
    (PRINT X)
    (PRINT Y))
```

just to be sure that everything was working correctly. When you use LEARN-FREQ, you will have to input the words of a piece of text in upper-case, and with a RETURN between each one. You can neaten up the input and display side of the program yourself some other time.

It is important to realise that you cannot just input a load of words from the dictionary and hope to produce a useful database. You must use a normal piece of common text. This ensures that the letter frequencies stored are those found distributed in text, and they can then be used to decode text.

FREQ-CHANGE

The function FREQ-CHANGE can now be defined, but first we will look at the data structure, and check that we agree on the actual storage method. Figure 7.3 shows the property list constructed here. The property in this case is called ATOTAL, and the identifiers are just the letters of the alphabet. Here, it is assumed that LEARN-FREQ has been running and thus some accumulated totals have already been made. To find the frequency so far of the letter E, for instance, you could type in:

```
(GET 'E 'ATOTAL)
```

which would return the value 15. Note that E and ATOTAL are QUOTEd as GET and PUT evaluate their arguments.

Alternatively, your LISP should have some equivalent of:

```
(PLIST 'E)
```

which will print all the properties of E, along with their values. If this is available, you should use it often in the following to inspect the present state of the letters' property lists.

property→ identifier↓	ATOTAL	...
A	13	
B	8	
C	1	
D	7	
E	15	
.		
.		
.		

Fig. 7.3 Letter frequency property list

FREQ-CHANGE takes two arguments, and changes the alphabet property given as the value of the first argument by calculating letter frequencies in the word given by the value of the second. Each letter in WORD is used as the identifier in a PUT and GET routine. The value to GET is the present value of ATOTAL for that letter, and the value to PUT back is the value plus one – i.e. incremented. This can be done recursively, starting with the case where WORD has one letter:

```
(DEFUN FREQ-CHANGE (PROP WORD)
   (COND ((NULL (CDR WORD))
          (PUT (CAR WORD) PROP
               (PLUS 1 (GET (CAR WORD) PROP))))
          ( . . . . . .
```

Remember that if WORD is a singleton, (CDR WORD) is NIL, and the single letter is (CAR WORD). Thus, when WORD is a singleton, the start of the function definition above performs a PUT, with the single letter in WORD as identifier. PROP contains the property to be changed, which will be ATOTAL when this function is called from LEARN-FREQ. The value to be PUT comes last, and this is 1 plus the previous value which is found from a GET function.

The next part of the recursion is an expression which assumes that FREQ-CHANGE works on CDR of WORD, and the final action is to complete it on CAR of WORD. These two operations are stated explicitly in a possible final definition as follows:

```
(DEFUN FREQ-CHANGE (PROP WORD)
   (COND ((NULL (CDR WORD))
          (PUT (CAR WORD) PROP
               (PLUS 1 (GET (CAR WORD) PROP))))
          (T (PUT (CAR WORD) PROP
                  (PLUS 1 (GET (CAR WORD) PROP)))
             (FREQ-CHANGE PROP (CDR WORD)))))
```

The expression following T in the COND list works on the CAR of WORD, and then calls FREQ-CHANGE to do the rest of WORD. It is this call which effectively reduces WORD by stripping off the head, and doing the whole function again. This iterates automatically until WORD is a singleton.

Now have a look at the definition above and think of what can be done to reduce it by omitting the repetition of one of the expressions. If you look at the two COND predicate pairs, one headed with a NULL and other by T, you can see that no matter which of these two alternatives is valid, the same PUT expression is always executed. This does not have to appear twice, it can simply be brought out and executed at the start of the definition, because it has to be executed whatever happens. In this case, the function simplifies by a reasonable amount to:

```
(DEFUN FREQ-CHANGE (PROP WORD)
    (PUT (CAR WORD) PROP (PLUS 1 (GET (CAR WORD) PROP)))
    (COND ((NULL (CDR WORD)))
          (T (FREQ-CHANGE PROP (CDR WORD)))))
```

This is a useful trick to remember, but will only work in cases such as this where the recursion is rather more trivial than in previous examples. Here, the recursion in the last line is only a question of calling up the function; the result does not actually have to be used for anything in that expression.

If you try using FREQ-CHANGE from scratch, the property values are not yet defined, and the GET returns NIL, which is not a numeric value, and an error occurs when PLUS tries to work on this. There are two obvious ways round this. The first is to include a trap for it in the function, and allow for it, the second is to set all the properties to zero before starting. We will use the latter as it might be useful for you to have a way of clearing the property list anyway, especially at the beginning when you are experimenting.

Before looking at using the above program, we will define a program for clearing the properties on the property list to zero.

Clearing the alphabet property list

This also brings up another point which can be cleared up for this program and for the decoding itself. How do you store the alphabet itself? Your LISP may be able to use ASCII codes, and generate the alphabet, but we will assume that it has to be stored verbatim. We will define the list ALPHABET using SETQ as:

```
(SETQ ALPHABET '(A B C D E F G H I J K L M N O
                 P Q R S T U V W X Y Z))
```

We can now store 0 against any property of ALPHABET which may be used by our programs. The zeroing function, called CLR, is defined to have two arguments. One is the list whose properties are being zeroed,

ALPHABET here, and the other is the property to be cleared, which will be ATOTAL when we call CLR shortly. The function can be defined recursively as follows:

```
(DEFUN CLR (INLIST PROP)
    (COND ((NULL INLIST) 'LIST-ZEROED)
          (T (PUT (CAR INLIST) PROP 0)
             (CLR (CDR INLIST) PROP))))
```

Defining CLR to have the arguments shown allows you to extend the application here to several property lists of several lists of letters.

Remember, also, that your LISP should have something like REMPROP which allows you to clear properties to the value NIL, or remove them altogether.

Using the above programs

To start off, you will have to clear the ATOTAL property of each member of the alphabet. This is done as follows:

```
(CLR ALPHABET 'ATOTAL)
```

The use of QUOTE for ATOTAL is slightly subtle here. If it is left out, it is the value of ATOTAL, and not ATOTAL itself which is zeroed. This means that when you run the CLR function, it finishes with the message LIST-ZEROED, and even does its job, after a fashion. When you try to use it in the previous functions, however, they fail because ATOTAL itself is still NIL. Try experimenting later, and try various GET expressions to see what happens.

Once CLR has been used, LEARN-FREQ can be run, and you will find that the messages are just adequate. You should neaten them up using your LISP's PRINT facilites later.

After using CLR, a short session with LEARN-FREQ will go something like:

```
EV: (LEARN-FREQ)
(INPUT WORDS WITH RETURNS)
(FINISH WITH XXX)

HELLO
THERE
XXX

Value : PROG-ENDS
```

You type in the function after the EV: prompt, and then HELLO THERE, with RETURNS, followed by XXX. The computer finishes with a value which is the last message to tell you that the program has finished.

The program will have changed the ATOTAL property of H,E,L,O,T and

R. It will have stored the number 3, for instance, under E, and the number 1 under R. To see these, use GET as follows:

```
(GET 'E 'ATOTAL)
(GET 'R 'ATOTAL)
```

The first will return 3, and the second 1.

General uses of frequency analysis

We now have a way of analysing text into letter frequencies, and the next step is to use this database to decode messages. However, the program above is interesting and quite useful on its own. You can produce a small printing program which will print out the alphabet with its associated frequencies of occurrence, and you can watch this database grow as you input more and more text. It is a true learning system. Furthermore, if you can SAVE the whole program with its database, you can call it up, use it, and not lose the knowledge when the computer is switched off.

You will find it interesting to write a short program to display the frequencies accumulated in the ATOTAL property, as text is input. This will also help you to understand the speed with which the learning process occurs, and how different types of text have different effects. Letter frequencies can be used for all sorts of applications other than message decoding. For instance, it might be instructive to try typing text from other languages, and see if you can detect a language purely from the pattern of frequencies of the letters. This might then be used as the first step in a generalised language translator which would recognise the languages of the people using it.

Letter frequencies in a piece of text can also give you indications of style. As a very simple example, if a piece of text has more than the usual relative frequency of I's in it, it is fair to assume that the writer is using the word I too much – the computer could prompt him to change his style.

The letter frequency programming principles lead onto word frequency, and this is an even better check on writing style. This type of overall watchdog activity would form a useful addition to a word processing program for children learning to write essays. The machine could point out simple style errors as they occur, which would be incomparably more valuable than explaining them later.

Message decoding

We will assume that the input coded message is contained in a list called MESSAGE, and that a function is to be defined called DECODE which takes in MESSAGE as its argument, and returns a list value equal to the decoded version. At the same time, DECODE will use the letter frequency of the words in MESSAGE to improve its own understanding of the code. In this way, DECODE learns to improve its performance as it is used more and more.

The first task is to work out the frequencies of letters occurring in MESSAGE, exactly as above. These can be stored on another property of the alphabet called CTOTAL. We will use LEARN-FREQ to accumulate higher and higher numbers in CTOTAL as MESSAGEs are input. You can always CLR the CTOTAL property, and start again whenever you wish. You will have to at the start anyway, for the same reason as before.

Once the message has been used to change CTOTAL, the next step is to compare relative frequencies of CTOTAL with those of ATOTAL. By this means, the appropriate letters can be associated together. The way in which this will be done here is described next.

Suppose the CTOTAL and ATOTAL properties have some values stored, and the next step is to decode the letters of the words in MESSAGE. The first step is to produce a list of the members of ALPHABET sorted into frequency order according to ATOTAL – that is, as they naturally occur in normal text. This list will be called ALPHANORM, and it will have, for instance, the most frequently occurring letter in its head. The next step is to do the same but using CTOTAL to produce ALPHACODE which also has the alphabet in descending order of frequency, but for the coded version.

Once we have these lists, we can strip the members off in pairs, one from each list, and thus form a translation between the code and the alphabet, or vice versa. It is possible, for instance, to add another property to the letters of the alphabet which is called CODELET which would store the coded version of each normal letter. We could also produce a property called NORMLET which would give the normal letter associated with each letter, assuming it to be in code. By these means, we produce a permanent record of the code. We can also wipe it when we wish, using CLR, or store several codes at once using properties such as CODELET1, NORMLET1 and CODELET2, NORMLET2, etc.

You can extend this at your leisure, for now we will look at programming DECODE, and we will use just NORMLET as described above.

Figure 7.4 shows a property list which we shall use in the following. It contains the properties mentioned above, and some typical entries. For instance, ATOTAL for A is 13, because it is a common letter, but CTOTAL is 0, signifying that A is code for a normal letter which is low in natural frequency such as X, which is shown as the NORMLET property. Thus, every time A is found in a coded message, it can be decoded to X. B, on the other hand, corresponds to a medium to low frequency letter such as H, C represents a very high frequency letter such as E, and so on. The CODELET property tells you how to code letters into a coded message. For instance, the word BAD would be coded to become TJF.

property→ identifier↓	ATOTAL	CTOTAL	CODELET	NORMLET
A	13	0	J	X
B	8	3	T	H
C	1	19	S	E
D	7	1	F	K
E	15	9	Y	A
.	.	.	.	.
.	.	.	.	.
.	.	.	.	.

Fig. 7.4   Full property list of alphabet

A map of the program

We have so far produced two separate programs, by giving three function definitions. The three functions are CLR, which is a separate program on its own, LEARN-FREQ and FREQ-CHANGE, which combine to form a program, headed LEARN-FREQ. This latter simply updates the frequencies of letters occurring in text. The next step is to consider the map of the decoding function itself. This is a fairly large LISP program, compared to previous examples, but you will see that we rarely define functions of more than a half dozen lines. This is the modularisation which LISP encourages.

Figure 7.5 shows a map of the complete application, including the two programs defined above. The map is set out to remind you of the program and function names, where they all fit in, and what type of arguments they take. DECODE uses several functions, and their names will be defined in the following. You can see the structure of DECODE from this map – it starts with an update on coded letter frequencies, it performs a sort on the alphabet, and finally it assembles the decoded word list. Keep this map in mind for the following.

One problem which you may encounter in the following is that of running out of memory space, especially if your computer has little to start with, and then loads the LISP interpreter into memory from disk or tape. You should not keep functions you do not need here, and you should maximise your available memory as much as possible. For instance, if using a BBC Micro-computer, or equivalent, use MODE 7 to run the program, to reduce the graphics to an absolute minimum, and release more memory.

Updating the CTOTAL property – CODE-FREQ

The first function to be produced updates the CTOTAL property. We will

(LEARN-FREQ)	Updates normal word frequencies
uses ↓	in the ATOTAL property of letters.
(FREQ-CHANGE prop. word)	Updates given property with letter frequencies in given word.
(CLR list prop.)	Zeros given property of given list.
┌─ (DECODE message) uses ↓	Returns decoded list.
└→ (CODE-FREQ message) uses ↓	Updates coded-letter frequencies in CTOTAL property of letters.
FREQ-CHANGE from above	
├→ (ALPHASORT list prop.) │ uses ↓	Sorts letters in list in descending order according to given property.
│ (ALPHASTONE list prop.)	Stones smallest member of list to end of list using given property.
└→ LEN & GEP	
└→ (WORD-SPLIT message) uses ↓	Assembles final decoded list.
(WORD-DECODE word)	Returns decoded words as a list of letters.

Fig. 7.5 Map of decoding functions

call it CODE-FREQ, and it uses the letters given in a coded message in the list MESSAGE. This will be similar to LEARN-FREQ, but takes its input from MESSAGE, instead of from the keyboard.

In fact, we can define CODE-FREQ recursively, and the definition simply strips the head off MESSAGE, EXPLODEs it and calls FREQ-CHANGE using ALPHABET and CTOTAL to update the coded frequencies.

To understand the following, recall that FREQ-CHANGE needs a property to update, followed by an exploded word from which to perform the updating.

The recursive definition of CODE-FREQ starts with the case where MESSAGE contains just one word. The CAR of MESSAGE is the only word to be acted upon, and can thus be EXPLODEd, and passed directly to FREQ-CHANGE. The next stage is to use CODE-FREQ for the CDR of MESSAGE, and add in the word in the CAR of MESSAGE to make it complete:

```
(DEFUN CODE-FREQ (MESSAGE)
    (COND ((NULL (CDR MESSAGE))
                     (FREQ-CHANGE 'CTOTAL
                            (EXPLODE (CAR MESSAGE))))
              (T (FREQ-CHANGE 'CTOTAL
                     (EXPLODE (CAR MESSAGE)))
              (CODE-FREQ (CDR MESSAGE))))))
```

Once again, there is an expression in the above which is needlessly repeated. The FREQ-CHANGE is performed whatever happens, and might as well be executed at the start of the program. The neater definition is as follows:

```
(DEFUN CODE-FREQ (MESSAGE)
    (FREQ-CHANGE 'CTOTAL (EXPLODE (CAR MESSAGE)))
    (COND ((NULL (CDR MESSAGE)))
              (T (CODE-FREQ (CDR MESSAGE)))))
```

This function is now complete, and we can update the CTOTAL of our database with messages to accumulate information on the code.

Sorting according to frequency – ALPHASORT

The next step is to produce alphabet lists for the code conversion, which comes from sorting the letters according to the real frequencies, ATOTAL, and the coded frequences, CTOTAL.

We will write a function which will act on the members of ALPHABET, and return a list containing those members sorted into descending order according to the values of one of the properties. We will call the function ALPHASORT. This function takes in the list to be sorted, and a property as its arguments. You can rewrite it to be more general if you wish, later.

The sort works exactly like DSORT. A special STONE function has to be written to move the letter with the smallest property value to the end of the list. The rewritten version of STONE is called ALPHASTONE, and it will take two arguments. These are the list to be sorted, and the property to be used as the sorting value. However, we will add one refinement to DSORT. Instead of using simply GREATERP in the comparison, we will use GEP, which is greater than or equal, and is defined as:

```
(DEFUN GEP (X Y)
    (NOT (LESSP X Y)) )
```

This saves the order of pairs of letters from being changed if they have the same value. The required function can now be defined as:

```
(DEFUN ALPHASTONE (SLIST PROP)
    (COND ((NULL (CDR SLIST)) SLIST)
              ((GEP (GET (CAR SLIST) PROP)
                     (GET (CADR SLIST) PROP))
                            (CONS (CAR SLIST)
```

```
                    (ALPHASTONE (CDR SLIST) PROP)))
    (T (CONS (CADR SLIST)
      (ALPHASTONE (CONS (CAR SLIST)
                        (CDDR SLIST)) PROP)))))
```

The only difference is that instead of comparing the actual values of the first two members of SLIST, it is the values of the given property which are compared. These values are, of course, fetched using GET.

Using ALPHASTONE is just as for STONE, and thus ALPHASORT follows DSORT exactly to give:

```
(DEFUN ALPHASORT (SLIST PROP)
  (SETQ N (LEN SLIST))
  (LOOP (UNTIL (EQ N 1) SLIST)
       (SETQ SLIST (ALPHASTONE SLIST PROP))
       (SETQ N (PLUS N -1))))
```

This function can now be tried out in full, and you should start by clearing the 'ATOTAL properties of ALPHABET so that you can see what is happening, and then use LEARN-FREQ to input some normal words. So type in:

```
(CLR ALPHABET 'ATOTAL)
```

and then:

```
(LEARN-FREQ)
```

followed by:

```
A
BB
CCC
DD
EEEE
XXX
```

This will store 1, 2, 3, 2, 4 against A, B, C, D and E in the 'ATOTAL property of these letters. Now type in:

```
(ALPHASORT ALPHABET 'ATOTAL)
```

and the program will respond with the alphabet sorted according to 'ATOTAL, with E, C, B, D and A at the start, and the rest of the alphabet in normal order following.

To see the coded part working, you will have to code a message, and store it in MESSAGE. Then use CODE-FREQ to adjust 'CTOTAL, and then ALPHASORT on 'CTOTAL instead of 'ATOTAL. This will produce the required order. We will have a go at an example when the DECODE program is complete.

DECODE

Remember, DECODE takes in MESSAGE, updates its knowledge of coded word frequencies, and returns the decoded version, or as near as it can. To do this it uses CODE-FREQ, and then ALPHASORT on 'ATOTAL and 'CTOTAL to produce two versions of the alphabet. One version, ALPHACODE, is the frequency-sorted version which results from analysing MESSAGE, and the other, ALPHANORM, is the result of using the normal letter frequencies for sorting. These two match up to give a transform from coded to decoded messages, or the other way round.

The best way to use this data is to store it as explained before, in a property of the letters. DECODE will need the NORMLET property filled in. This gives a quick and easy method of tying up coded letters with normal letters.

DECODE then takes each letter in MESSAGE, and matches it up with the normal letter to produce the decoded version of MESSAGE.

The first time DECODE is used, it relies on MESSAGE being large enough to be able to find the frequencies for coded letters accurately enough to perform the matching properly. The program is designed to allow as many messages as you like to be input, and it will learn to perform the decoding more and more accurately as it is given more and more data. DECODE also depends upon enough normal text having been input for the machine to know the actual frequencies accurately. At a later date you can refine it to do things such as looking for all single-letter words, to decide whether they are A or I. For now, we will produce a fairly rudimentary program for general interest.

The program starts with:

```
(DEFUN DECODE (MESSAGE)
  (CODE-FREQ MESSAGE)
  (SETQ ALPHACODE (ALPHASORT ALPHABET 'CTOTAL))
  (SETQ ALPHANORM (ALPHASORT ALPHABET 'ATOTAL))
  ( . . . . . .
```

This updates the database, and produces the two versions of the alphabet sorted in frequency order in ALPHACODE and ALPHANORM for coded and normal text respectively. The next step is to store this matching in the NORMLET property of the letters. This means that each letter of ALPHACODE has its NORMLET property set equal to its opposite number in ALPHANORM. This can be done using the following type of loop:

```
(LOOP (UNTIL (NULL ALPHANORM))
      (PUT (CAR ALPHACODE) 'NORMLET (CAR ALPHANORM))
      (SETQ ALPHACODE (CDR ALPHACODE))
      (SETQ ALPHANORM (CDR ALPHANORM)))
```

This loop actually destroys ALPHACODE and ALPHANORM, but you can prevent this from happening with a little thought, and this is left to you as an exercise if you need these two lists for something else.

Decoding words – WORD-SPLIT and WORD-DECODE

Now we can decode MESSAGE at last! This will be split up into two functions so that we can use recursion. The outer function is called WORD-SPLIT, and the inner is called WORD-DECODE. WORD-SPLIT takes the words of MESSAGE one at a time, passes them to WORD-DECODE to be decoded, and assembles them into a list – the final decoded list.

WORD-SPLIT is defined first. It takes MESSAGE, and returns a list of the decoded version. It starts off with the single word case, and decodes the head. It then assumes that the CDR of MESSAGE has been done, and adds on the decoded version of the head. The decode of the head is done whatever the outcome of the COND, and thus it is done first in the function. The whole function can be written as:

```
(DEFUN WORD-SPLIT (MESSAGE)
  (RPLACA
     MESSAGE
       (IMPLODE (WORD-DECODE (EXPLODE (CAR MESSAGE)))))
  (COND ((NULL (CDR MESSAGE)) MESSAGE)
        (T (CONS (CAR MESSAGE)
                 (WORD-SPLIT (CDR MESSAGE))))))
```

In this function the head word of the local variable MESSAGE is replaced with the decoded version before the rest of the function is performed. Note that WORD-DECODE works with a list containing the letters of the given word, and hence the EXPLODE and IMPLODE functions. MESSAGE is then checked to see if it is a singleton. If so, the process is complete. The recursion simply puts the decoded head of MESSAGE back onto the decoded CDR of MESSAGE.

WORD-DECODE is performed by taking the given word, as a list of letters, and changing each letter to the letter found in NORMLET. The word is then handed back as a list. Using recursion, this function is defined as follows:

```
(DEFUN WORD-DECODE (WORD)
  (RPLACA WORD (GET (CAR WORD) 'NORMLET))
  (COND ((NULL (CDR WORD)) WORD)
        (T (CONS (CAR WORD) (WORD-DECODE (CDR WORD))))))
```

The first function automatically replaces the CAR of WORD with the decoded version, and the COND checks to see if WORD is a singleton. When it is, the function ceases. The recursion assumes WORD-DECODE to work on the CDR of WORD, and the decoded CAR is then added on.

The final decoding program

The complete version of DECODE is as follows:

```
(DEFUN DECODE (MESSAGE)
  (CODE-FREQ MESSAGE)
  (SETQ ALPHACODE (ALPHASORT ALPHABET 'CTOTAL))
  (SETQ ALPHANORM (ALPHASORT ALPHABET 'ATOTAL))
  (LOOP (UNTIL (NULL ALPHANORM))
        (PUT (CAR ALPHACODE) 'NORMLET (CAR ALPHANORM))
        (SETQ ALPHACODE (CDR ALPHACODE))
        (SETQ ALPHANORM (CDR ALPHANORM)))
  (WORD-SPLIT MESSAGE))
```

As you can see from here and from Figure 7.5 it uses three main functions, which have two or three subfunctions. Despite the complexity of the application, the program is quite short, and splits into enough small parts to make it possible to read through the definition without too much trouble.

This is made possible by a number of the attributes of LISP. Firstly, it is well fitted for list manipulation, so there is little to synthesise from scratch of a simple house-keeping nature. Secondly, LISP allows recursion – the program would be quite a bit longer and more involved using just LOOP. Thirdly, the functional storage method of LISP allows the flexibility to define new commands internally, and it is not necessary to carry their definitions about and place them explicitly into every program which uses them. This allows a sort of summary of the total process, like the definition of DECODE above, which does not cloud its working by defining each separate part within DECODE itself.

Most of the above features can be used or synthesised using the imperative languages such as BASIC, but none of them will produce such neat and pleasing-looking routines for list processing applications.

Using the program

Using the above involves spending some time typing normal text into the LEARN-FREQ program. The text is input in upper-case, separated word by word by RETURNs; if you type in two words with a space between, LISP will normally ignore the second. You will find it easier to input several words at once as a continuous stream of letters, without spaces, and followed by RETURN. It is only the letters that LEARN-FREQ is interested in. Finish with XXX.

This will set up the normal database, and allow the comparison to be made. The more words input at this stage the better. You will not find that the decoding improves dramatically until the word frequencies are reasonably correct. This is because a wrong letter at the front of the ordered letter lists will put several others out. Thus, it is important to input as much normal and coded text as possible.

To test the decoder, CLR 'ATOTAL and 'CTOTAL, to give a clean slate, and work out some coded text. The easiest code is simply to move each letter up (or down) by one letter. For instance, coding the words HELLO THERE could be done as:

HELLO THERE
IFMMP UIFSF

Each letter in the code is the next one up from its normal version.

The two uncoded words should be typed into LEARN-FREQ, and then DECODE should be called up as:

```
(DECODE '(IFMMP UIFSF))
```

This will yield (HELLO THERE). This is a completely artificial example, of course; we are feeding it with the same words whether coded or uncoded, and the two ordered listings of the alphabet will always be the same, and will simply decode perfectly. To see where a departure occurs, code the list (THIS WORKS) to give (UIJT XPSLT). Now type the coded version into DECODE without typing the correct version into LEARN-FREQ. The result is (AHBT DORCT). Remember that the database is continuously updating itself, and you should be careful not to type the same thing into DECODE more than once, unless part of normal text, or the database will form a lop-sided view of word frequencies in normal text.

To see the effects of this, code up

(ZEALOUS HAZY SIZZLING JAZZY FEZ)

and feed into DECODE without using LEARN-FREQ. Note that Z here is replaced by A in code. Now try typing the code for (HELLO THERE) into DECODE again. It is no longer correct because the program has adjusted all the previous letter frequencies to take account of the phrase input above, which it believes is normal text.

The only solution to the problem of incorrect decoding by this type of program is to input a lot of normal text. This ensures that a small amount of out-of-character input from time to time has little effect.

You can now experiment with the software and imagine ways of improving it. When you think of one, remember the lessons learnt in this example. Write the function you wish to perform as a set of functions, and worry about how to define the lower ones after you are happy with the philosophy of the higher functions.

Appendix One
Standard LISP Functions

Introduction

This Appendix is an alphabetical list of the functions described in this book. All the usual cautionary notes apply about different LISP dialects, but the following shows how the functions will be assumed to be defined here. Some extra functions are also described which are defined in terms of the others, but are considered important, and may be included on your LISP as standard functions already.

All functions below evaluate their arguments, and do not alter them, unless otherwise stated.

(AND A B C D . . .) A Boolean function which can take any number of arguments, each of which is a predicate. AND returns T if all of its arguments are T, and NIL otherwise.

(APPEND list list) This is defined in the book in terms of standard LISP functions. The function takes two list arguments, and produces the list containing the union of the lists – in the same order as their appearance in APPEND.

(APPLY fn list) This function takes a function and a list as arguments. The list must contain a single valid set of arguments for the given function, and APPLY applies that function to the arguments in the given list.

(ASSOC index list) This function returns the list member of the given list which has the index as its head.

(ATOM A) This returns T if A is an atom, NIL otherwise.

(CAR list) This returns the head of the list.

(CDR list) This returns the tail of the list – always a list value.

(CADR list) applies CDR then CAR to list.

(CDDR list) applies CDR then CDR to list.

Further functions of this type can be made up by using up to three D's and A's between C and R.

(COND (predicate expression)
       (predicate expression)
       (. . .
       (. . .

The above COND function evaluates only that expression which follows the first true predicate in one of the predicate pairs above. The COND then ceases without evaluating any further. The COND returns the value of the evaluated expression.

(CONS A B) This dots A onto B. For instance, if A is an atom, and B a list, CONS forms a new list containing A followed by the members of B.

(DEFUN function-name list A B C . .) The list contains the (evaluated) arguments for the function named in the first argument. The remaining arguments of DEFUN form the function definition. In this book, it is assumed that if the second argument is not a list, then it must be an identifier which is bound to a list of the arguments used in calling the function. These arguments are not automatically evaluated. The value returned by the defined function is equal to the last item evaluated before finishing.

(DIFFERENCE A B) subtracts integer B from integer A.

(EDIT A) See Appendix 2.

(EQ A B) returns T if A and B are equal atoms or, if they are identical lists, is stored in the same place.

(EQUAL A B) As defined in this book, it returns T if A and B are EQ, or if they are lexically identical lists.

EV: is short for EVAL (see below). This is the computer prompt which is assumed in this book.

(EVAL A) This function evaluates A, and returns the result. EVAL is running all the time in your LISP interpreter, and anything you type potentially has a value for which EVAL is searching. If it finds an atom it prints out its value, or tells you it is undefined. If it finds a list, it looks at the head, assumes it is a function name, and looks for its definition. It will assume that the rest of the items in the list are the arguments of the function in the head.

(EXPLODE A) returns a list containing the characters of the identifier A.

(GET identifier property) returns the value of the property attached to the given identifier.

(GREATERP A B) returns T if integer A is greater than integer B, NIL otherwise.

(IMPLODE A) removes the spaces between the items in the list A, opposite to EXPLODE.

(LAMBDA list A B C . . .) the same as for DEFUN, but not bound to a function name.

(LESSP A B) returns T if integer A is less than B, NIL otherwise.

(LIST A B C . . .) returns a list containing its arguments as members.

(LISTP A) returns T if A is a list, NIL otherwise.

(LOAD A) may be the function which recalls a complete memory image of a LISP session from your disk or tape, with name equal to the value of A.

(LOOP A B C . . .) will continually repeat the evaluation of the expressions in its arguments until stopped by an error, UNTIL or WHILE. LOOP returns the value of the last item evaluated before leaving the loop.

(MAPC fn list) This function applies the function in the second argument to each of the members of the given list, and returns a list of the outcomes.

(MINUSP A) returns T if the integer A is negative, NIL otherwise.

NIL A LISP constant meaning FALSE or empty.

(NOT A) returns T if A is NIL, and vice versa.

(NULL A) returns T if A has value NIL, NIL otherwise.

(NUMBERP A) returns T if A is a number, NIL otherwise.

(ONEP A) returns T if A has the value 1, NIL otherwise.

(OR A B C . . .) returns T upon evaluating an argument with value T. It does not evaluate the rest of the arguments. Returns NIL otherwise.

(PLIST identifier) prints out the complete set of properties of the identifier with their values.

(PLUS A B) returns the sum of integers A and B.

(PRINT A) may take multiple arguments. It simply prints the value of the argument to the screen.

(PUT identifier property value) stores the value to the property of the identifier's property list – all arguments are evaluated, as for most other functions.

(QUOTE A) tells EVAL not to evaluate the argument, but return it literally – one of the few functions which does not evaluate its argument. Can be replaced by a single QUOTE, as in: 'A. (This is equal to the letter A, and not the value of the atom A.)

(QUOTIENT A B) returns integer A divided by integer B, and will normally round off towards zero to return an integer.

(READ) returns the next item typed to the keyboard, and ended with RETURN. Will only return the first item if several are typed in and separated with spaces. However, a list of object may be typed in, if enclosed in round brackets. The typed input is not evaluated, it is taken literally, and does not need to be quoted.

(REMAINDER A B) returns the integer remainder on division of integer A by integer B.

(REMPROP identifier property) removes (or sets to NIL) the given property of the given identifier.

(RPLACA list B) actually changes the first argument's value by replacing its head with B. This is the primary action of the function, though it also returns a value, which may be anything depending upon your LISP dialect. We assume, here, that it returns the new list value of the first argument.

(RPLACD list B) is as for RPLACA, but replaces the CDR of the first argument with B.

(SAVE A) may be the function which allows you to store the present state of memory to a disk or cassette file with name equal to the value of A.

(SET A B) actually changes the first argument by setting the identifier found as the value of A to the value of B.

(SETQ A B) is the same as SET, but does not evaluate its first argument; thus it sets A itself to the value of B.

T   A LISP constant signifying a TRUE value.

(TIMES A B) returns the product of integer A and integer B.

(UNTIL predicate A B C . .) is used to terminate a LOOP function. When the predicate has the value T, the loop ends, but evaluates the arguments of UNTIL before leaving the loop. The last one evaluated is returned as the value of the LOOP function.

(WHILE predicate A B C . . .) is used to terminate a loop. When the predicate is NIL, the loop ends by evaluating the rest of the arguments in the WHILE. The last one evaluated gives its value to the LOOP function.

(ZEROP A) returns T if A equals 0, NIL otherwise.

Appendix Two
Editing – The Acornsoft LISP Editor

Introduction

The process of editing is highly machine-specific as well as depending upon the LISP version which is run. However, it is very helpful to be able to edit a function definition after it has been written. As LISP has no line numbers, this task is usually rather difficult. Editing on your LISP may rely on standard EDIT programs, and they vary quite considerably. This makes the description of editing generally rather difficult to attempt. This Appendix chooses one such editor, and shows you how to use it – the Acornsoft LISP editor. It is a very LISP-like editor, and relies upon your knowing LISP quite well. You should not try to read the following until you have at least read and tried the examples of Chapter 3.

In the following explanations you should follow the instructions with great care, as they are designed to construct lists in a particular way. If you deviate even by a small amount, you may miss an important point.

Editing

This editor relies upon the fact that the function definition under consideration is simply a list. Chapter 6 explains how functions are normally stored. They are stored as lists with the word LAMBDA at their head, and with no reference to the function name used to call them up. Thus, the function defined as:

```
(DEFUN FN1   (X Y Z)
   (SETQ X (PLUS Y (PLUS Y Z)))
   (PRINT X)
   (SETQ X (LIST Y Z)))
```

is actually stored as:

```
(LAMBDA (X Y Z)
   (SETQ X (PLUS Y (PLUS Y Z)))
   (PRINT X)
   (SETQ X (LIST Y Z)))
```

You will have to accept this until you have read Chapter 6.

As you can see, the second version of the function definition above has five elements, all of which are lists except for LAMBDA. The second member is the list (X Y Z); the remaining three are SETQ function lists. Thus each item in the definition above has a description in such terms as 'the third member' or the 'second member of the third member' – all good clean list manipulation statements which can be approached using CAR, CDR and their derivatives. For instance, you should be able to see that the CAR of the CDDR of the definition is SETQ. By this means we can extract any part of the definition. This is the principle behind the Acornsoft editor. There are six commands, plus the use of the RETURN key. The six commands allow any part of a function definition to be acted upon, or any part of the definition to be added to with further elements.

To see how it works, you type in:

```
(EDIT FN1)
```

The screen then shows something like:

```
(LAMBDA
    (X Y Z)
    (SETQ
        X
        (PLUS Y (PLUS Y Z)))
    (PRINT X)
    (SETQ X (LIST Y Z)))
```

This method of indenting to highlight the hierarchy or level of each part of the code is called 'pretty printing', and is very useful indeed in viewing the expressions. Brackets which start in the same vertical column are at the same bracket level. Thus all members of FN1's function definition list are on the same level except for the LAMBDA, which is considered to be a function placed at the head of its argument list.

At any time, you can press RETURN and the current list or expression which the editor is working on will be displayed. Thus the above is repeated on the screen if you press RETURN. You should think of the editor working on this list as if it has a pointer which it can move about. The commands are as follows:

A moves the pointer to the CAR of the present expression. Try pressing A, followed by RETURN. This causes LAMBDA to be printed, because that is the CAR of the present expression being looked at by the editor. If you press RETURN again, it will simply print out the present expression, which is LAMBDA, again.

B moves the editor pointer up one level. Try typing B without RETURN. Believe it or not, B has had an effect, but you cannot tell until you press RETURN and view the current expression. Try it! You can see that the editor has moved up in the hierarchy to the start again.

D moves the editor pointer to the CDR of the current expression. Press D, and try to predict the effect it has had before viewing it with RETURN. The CDR of the present expression is everything but the LAMBDA, and it is all printed out as a list – note the extra pair of brackets around the whole expression. Now try typing in DD. This will execute D twice, but you will see nothing until RETURN is pressed. Try to predict, once again, the effect, and then press RETURN.

The effect of this last command was to move the pointer to the CDR of the CDR of the list. Thus the PRINT and last SETQ are now showing. Now try typing BB to move back again.

So far we have tried moving around the file, and exposing the CAR of the current expression. Each time, you were told that the command was being executed, but you could not see it until RETURN was pressed. If you did not believe this, try typing in BB, without RETURN, and you will be convinced.

This causes the edit pointer to move up two places in the hierarchy – but there is only one left at this point, and the editor falls off the end of the list, comes out of EDIT, and prints a value, as LISP always must. The value is simply the definition list of FN1, without being 'pretty printed'.

Now return to editing FN1, by using EDIT. There are *three* commands for actually changing the data in the list, and these are as follows:

C inserts an expression at the head of the current expression. It acts immediately, and if you are at the start of the list now, type C. The cursor jumps to the next line, and you are expected to type in the item you wish to be placed at the head of the current expression. Type in HHH, and press RETURN to see what you have done. You will see that the editor has blindly added this before the LAMBDA in the list.

X removes the head of the current list. Try it now, and then press RETURN – the list is returned to normal. Remember, you can press RETURN whenever you like, to view the current expression if you are lost.

R is a very drastic function – use it with care. It replaces the current expression, completely, with whatever you type in next. Do not use it yet. Type in DDD and press RETURN. You should be able to see that the PRINT expression is at the head of the current expression. Type A and a RETURN. This gives the PRINT expression itself, and if you now type R, this is executed immediately, and the cursor jumps to the next line, awaiting your pleasure. Type HELLO followed by RETURN. This will replace the PRINT with an unbracketed atom called HELLO.

Press B a couple of times to see the new atom in context. Now press A again, and replace the current expression with HELLO again. This should have replaced something else in the list. Press B just twice more, RETURN, and view our handywork. Now press ESCAPE. This removes you from EDIT, and to look at the effect of our last few actions, just EDIT FN1 again, and you should have a pleasant surprise. The HELLOs are gone, along with any other changes you might have made in the last EDITing session – any made before, however, will still be there.

Leaving EDIT

You now know two ways of leaving EDIT. If you use B until the edit ceases, the whole list is printed out, and all changes are preserved in that session. If you press ESCAPE, the editor is exited, but all changes made in that session are lost.

Moving about in the function

Either EDIT FN1 back to its original definition, or redefine it from scratch and enter EDIT to arrive at the LAMBDA list version of FN1 at the start of this appendix.

Try typing DDDD – four D's. If you look at the screen, four D's brings you to the last SETQ member of the list, but remember that D simply takes the CDR each time, and thus it must return a list on each occasion, as there are no dotted pairs here. If you press RETURN now, the last member of the list is printed as a singleton member of the current expression which is a list. There are thus two sets of brackets around the SETQ expression. Thus CAR of this is the SETQ list itself – try typing in A and RETURN. One set of brackets is removed and the CAR is printed. It also happens to be a list in this case.

Now type in B again, and RETURN. This brings you back to the list with a single member. Try typing in D again, followed by RETURN. The answer, as you should expect, is NIL, because a singleton list has only one member, and thus the CDR is empty. Now type in B three times, and RETURN. It should be clear to you that if you now type in D four times, you will fall off the edge of the list. Try it without using RETURN – the editor accepts the instructions, but the last D is illegal, and it types out an asterisk after the last D to signify this. The instruction is ignored, as you can see by typing RETURN and looking at the NIL in the CDR of the singleton containing the last SETQ list.

Altering the function

Return to the top of the function again. We will now add some new parts to the definition. For instance, if you look at the second PLUS function in the first SETQ list, its first argument is Y. Can you change it to Z? Have a try!

The first task is make the Y the current expression; you can then work on it. Use D twice, and look at the result. This has the first SETQ as the CAR of the current expression, thus you must press A. This is a list again, and if you use D twice again, you arrive at a singleton list containing one member. If you press D again, you will arrive at the NIL at the end of the list. Try it, you can always press B after that and return to where you were. Now press A to enter the single member of the current expression. This gives a list of three elements. They are (a) the atom PLUS (b) the atom Y (c) the list (PLUS Y Z).

It is the last item that you want to enter. Do two D's, and you are at the singleton list containing the PLUS list as its member. You will have to use A to enter that inner list. Now you have three members again, and it is the second member which is to be changed. D followed by A will isolate the Y, without any brackets, and it then becomes the current expression, and can be replaced using R followed by Z and RETURN. Or, when you arrived at (Y Z), you could have deleted the CAR of the current expression, which would have removed Y. You can then use C to insert a new head – Z.

Now use B followed by RETURN several times, and watch the function gradually reappear as we return up the hierarchy. Remember, to preserve these changes simply continue using B until you fall off the top.

Conclusion

The secret of the editor is continuously to think of the function definition as a list, and D and A as CDR and CAR respectively. If you remember this, you will find it easy to use the editor, even though there are some tricky situations which you may find difficult to solve.

To use the editor to its full, you should now try some tricky changes to FN1, such as adding new expressions to the definition to extend it some way.

Index

Index